# God's Will

# YOU HEALED

## Chad Gonzales

AUXANO
PUBLICATIONS

ISBN
978-0-9777380-1-4

# Contents

# Preface

For centuries people have questioned God's willingness to heal. God's ability has seldom been questioned, yet His willingness has always been a debatable topic. Tradition and religion have not helped in the least bit; these two companions have only furthered people's ignorance about God's willingness to heal.

As the years go by, it astounds me as to how many people sincerely do not know the truth about God's will concerning healing. We live in a time like no other. We have had an explosion of revelation concerning God's Word over the last 30 years; yet, the vast majority of society knows nothing about God's Word. As a result, people do not know God's will concerning healing, for God's Word is His will.

Instead of taking man's word or basing our beliefs on our experiences, let us once and for all throw aside tradition, take religion to the curb, trash experiences and grasp the Word of God like never before. As you go through this book and study guide, you will clearly see that this is not based on my opinions or experiences, but based on the Word of God.

In my ministry, I endeavor to let the Bible speak for itself and so I give my listeners plenty of scripture to back up what is being said. Jesus said that by the mouth of two or three witnesses every word is established. Well, I like to say that by the mouth of two or three scriptures every belief will be established. I have found if there is a truth in the Bible God wants us to grasp, there will be more than just one scripture or little passage regarding that truth.

What we have done in this book is give you multiple Bible based reasons why it is God's will for you to be healed. The more evidence you have, the greater your foundation of faith will be concerning healing and the bolder you will be in your convictions.

Join with me as we discover the truth about God's will concerning healing. May the Holy Spirit lead you, guide you and direct you in your study and give you supernatural insight and understanding. Let us finally comprehend and forever settle with absolute certainty that God's will is you healed!

# Chapter 1

# Where Did You Get Those Beliefs?

People get themselves into a great deal of trouble when they establish their beliefs about God based on their experiences. I know of so many people who are mad at God because of a bad experience in life. They can not figure out why their mother died young, their friend became blind because of an accident or a close friend died of a chronic disease; therefore, they simply blame God.

Other people base their beliefs about God solely on what they heard a preacher say, especially if the preacher is on television. Please understand - anyone can be on television if they have enough money and anyone can call themselves a preacher and anyone can give themselves a title. Just because someone gets on Christian television and calls themselves an "apostle-prophet-bishop" of the "Running With Jesus Holy Sanctified Baptist Church" - that doesn't mean squat. Just because they have expensive clothes and flashy jewelry - that doesn't mean diddley squat. Just because they call themselves Dr. so and so and have all kinds of initials after their name - that has about as much value as a rotten apple if they are not speaking the Truth.

People need to stop letting false ministers with exceptional people skills, flashy attire, fancy words, ten dollar diplomas and five dollar credentials pull the wool over their heads. Little Red Riding Hood was smart enough to recognize that it was a wolf pretending to be her grandma; some of us haven't been so smart! It would do you good to pull the mask off some of these so called ministers and recognize the devil trying to rob you of God's blessings. God does use people to reveal and teach you truths; that is the whole purpose of the five-fold ministry gifts (the apostle, prophet, evangelist, pastor, and teacher)  but what they say must line up with the Word!

Your beliefs are to be founded, established and maintained by the Word of God (2 Timothy 3:16.) If what any preacher says, including me, doesn't line up with God's Word - you need to trash it. Romans 10:17 states, "Faith comes by hearing and hearing the Word of God." True Bible faith is simply trusting and relying on God. Well, how do you obtain faith in God's promises? By hearing His Word.

In John 6:63, Jesus said, "My Words are truth and they are life." God's Word will always bear witness with your spirit and it will always bring life to you. God said in Romans 8:14 that we are to be led by His Spirit and yet multitudes of people are being led by experiences, by a so called prophet, or by the words of a 21 day self-help book.

Jesus said in John 14 that the Holy Spirit only says what He hears; thus, the Holy Spirit only speaks what God says. In essence, the Holy Spirit will always and I mean always lead you in line with the Word of God. The Holy Spirit is your Teacher and He will guide you into all truth. As far as He is concerned, there is only one truth:  the Word of God.

In summary, your beliefs are to be built upon the Word of God.  If you want to know about God and the way He thinks and operates, just look to His Word.  You will see in a later chapter that within God's written Word, you can look at Jesus, the Living Word, and see how God truly speaks, acts, thinks, feels and operates.

# Chapter 2

# I Know You Can, But Will You?

Since the days of Jesus, people have asked this question to God. Very rarely will you find someone who doesn't believe that God is powerful enough to heal; instead, you find that people are wondering if God will heal. A common statement heard all around the world is, "God might heal them, but I don't know if He will heal me."

In Matthew 8, we find a wonderful story revealing God's willingness to heal.

> *1* When He had come down from the mountain, great multitudes followed Him. *2* And behold, a leper came and worshiped Him, saying, "Lord, if You are willing, You can make me clean." *3* Then Jesus put out His hand and touched him, saying, "I am willing; be cleansed." Immediately his leprosy was cleansed.
>
> **Matthew 8:1-3**

In all of the recorded healings in the ministry of Jesus, this was the only individual who came to Jesus for healing, yet was unsure if Jesus would heal. Just like this leper, so many in the world do not doubt that God can heal, but sincerely question if He will. I find it very interesting that in all those who came to Jesus for healing, this individual was the only one Jesus had to correct before He could heal him.

*You see, it is not enough to know God's ability; you must also know His will.* Faith in God's ability is simply not enough; faith alone in God's ability will not get you healed. You must know that God is *able* to heal and that He *will* heal; this is one of the basis for healing. Let me give you an example. Suppose you were in a conference of five hundred people and Bill Gates was the speaker. Bill Gates stands before the audience and states, "I have the ability to give each one of you one thousand dollars before you leave today." Would that cause you to get excited? With Bill Gates being one of the richest people in the world, you certainly know he is capable of giving away five hundred thousand dollars.

The problem with the situation is: you don't know if he will. You would sit there and wonder, "I know he can give me one thousand dollars; I just wonder if He will?" Without knowing if he is willing to give you the money, you have no reason to be excited; you have no reason to expect to receive it. Yet, if Bill Gates stood up and said, "Before you leave this conference, I am going to give each of you one thousand dollars" then you have every right to be excited and walk up to him with confidence and ask for your one thousand dollars.

In the same way, in order for you to believe God for healing, you must know that it is His will for you to be healed. When you know that God can and then you know that He will, you have the right ingredients for faith. Throughout the rest of this book, we are going to look at various scriptures that prove without a doubt that God's desire and plan is for you to be totally free of sickness and disease.

# Chapter 3
# God Good. Devil Bad.

In order to understand the will of God concerning healing, we must know the source of sickness, disease and death. Many people say these all come from God; even insurance companies call natural disasters "acts of God." My first question is, "What scripture are you basing your opinion on?" My second question is, "If God is doing all these horrible things, what is Satan doing?"

Everyone has an opinion about the Bible; rarely does anyone have scripture to back their opinion. Most people base their opinions or beliefs on life experiences or what some uninformed, ignorant person told them about God.

The vast majority of the world believes in Satan, but most of them do not know what he is doing. If everyone thinks God is sending sickness on people, killing people, and destroying families, what do they think Satan is doing -roasting marshmallows around the lake of fire?

Do you want to know where sickness and disease come from? Do you want to know where death comes from? Good news...I have the answer! I like to put it in a very simple way I call Sesame Street style. Are you ready? Here it is: "God good. Devil bad."

If you will learn this simple truth, it will help you in your

Bible studies and help you differentiate between what is of God and what is of the devil. Now let me show you some scriptures to back up this statement. Let us first look at a statement Jesus made in the book of John.

> **10 The thief does not come except to steal, and to kill, and to destroy. I have come that they may have life, and that they may have it more abundantly.**
>
> John 10:10

Here Jesus gives us a direct contrast of His activities and Satan's activities. Jesus said He gives people life and Satan steals, kills, and destroys. Well, does sickness steal? Does sickness kill? Does sickness destroy? You better believe it does!

Sickness and disease steals your money. You have to pay good money for doctor appointments, prescriptions, insurance co-pays, etc. Sickness and disease can kill you. Even the most minor illnesses left untreated can open the door to more serious illnesses which can take your life.

Sickness can not only destroy lives, but it can also destroy marriages and families. I have seen families fall apart because a loved one died. Marriages have been destroyed because one spouse could not handle the stress and burden of their child having a long lasting terminal disease. Families have gone bankrupt simply trying to pay medical bills.

So if something steals, kills, and destroys, then Jesus did not bring it. Jesus said He gives life. Does healing bring life? Yes! Healing gives, puts back together and builds up. Healing brings life!

Someone with half a brain could tell you that sickness, disease and death does not bring life. It doesn't make you prosper, it doesn't bring joy, and it doesn't build you up. So, according to this scripture, sickness, disease and death come from the devil; healing comes from Jesus.

Here is another scripture which goes right along with John 10:10.

**38 How God anointed Jesus of Nazareth with the Holy Spirit and with power, who went about doing good and healing all who were oppressed by the devil, for God was with Him.**

**Acts 10:38**

For me, John 10:10 and Acts 10:38 settle with finality who brings sickness and Who brings health. Notice what it says here: Jesus went about doing good and healing. Who was doing the healing? Jesus. Also, look at Who was working with Jesus? God and the Holy Ghost! So you have God, Jesus, and the Holy Ghost all working together healing people. Did you notice who was oppressing people with sickness? Yep, that stupid devil!

This scripture also blows away the misconception that Satan and God work together. Now please explain to me, with this scripture in mind, how anyone could say that Satan works with God to make people sick? Not according to this scripture! God is healing people and the devil is making people sick. God is bringing people to life and the devil is trying to kill them. In short, God good...devil bad.

Get a hold of this! This will help straighten out your beliefs and will help you straighten out other people's beliefs.

Anytime a person tells you that God put cancer on someone, show them Acts 10:38 and see what they have to say! I guarantee it will shut them up!

Either the Bible is true or it's a lie. Which one is it? I choose to believe the Bible, the whole Bible - which includes John 10:10 and Acts 10:38. They both tell me that Satan is a scuzzbucket because he makes people sick and kills people; yet they also tell me that Jesus heals and brings life to people!

> *14* **Forasmuch then as the children are partakers of flesh and blood, he also himself likewise took part of the same; that through death he might destroy him that had the power of death, that is the devil.**
>
> **Hebrews 2:14**

Where does death come from? The devil. Death comes from the devil. Who came to destroy death? Jesus! Can sickness and disease kill you? Yes it can. Sickness and disease can ultimately lead to death. Satan is the author of death; therefore, he is the author of sickness.

I have more scriptures to prove to you that God is good and the devil is bad. The only way to get rid of faulty thinking is to fill up with truths from the Word. Let's look at James 1:17.

> *17* **Every good gift and every perfect gift is from above, and comes down from the Father of lights, with whom there is no variation or shadow of turning.**
>
> **James 1:17**

Notice, every good and perfect gift comes down from God. Is sickness good? Is disease good? Is death good? No! No! No! Sickness is bad. If sickness were a good thing, then why do we have so many doctors, hospitals, clinics, etc? It is because sickness is bad and no one wants it!

Is healing good? Is health good? Is wholeness good? Yes! Yes! Yes! According to James 1:17 every good and perfect gift comes from God; so, we know that sickness and disease can not come from God! God is the Healer! He is a good God!

Romans 2:4 is a wonderful scripture about the goodness of God and what it does for mankind.

**4 Or do you despise the riches of His goodness, forbearance, and longsuffering, not knowing that the goodness of God leads you to repentance?**
**Romans 2:4**

Again, is sickness good? No. Well, if sickness is a part of the goodness of God, then that would mean that sickness brings people to Jesus. What if someone covered in boils, with a runny nose, blood shot eyes and a big goiter on their neck came up to you and said, "If you accept Jesus, you can be like me!" Would you be compelled to come to Jesus? No, you would be compelled to run away!

Who wants a Jesus who makes people sick? No one! But people do want a Jesus who can make them well. That's why Romans 2:4 says it's the goodness of God that brings men to repentance. Healing is good! Sickness is bad!

Did you ever notice how many people came running to Jesus for healing? Multitudes! *Did you ever notice how many people ran out to the leper camps to get some free leprosy? Not a single one!* Common sense will do you a lot of good!

If you read throughout the Gospels, you will see very quickly that because of the numerous healings in the ministry of Jesus, multitudes began believing on Him. Because of the goodness of God, masses of people turned from their sinful ways and turned to God.

Remember: God good; devil bad. This simple truth will help you and keep you. If anything good happens in your life, it's of God. If anything bad happens in your life, it's of the devil.

God doesn't bring disaster. God doesn't bring disease. God doesn't bring tornadoes, hurricanes or hail storms. He doesn't send cancer, pneumonia, arthritis or heart attacks. God sends life because He is life! If God was to give you cancer, He would have to steal it from the devil because God doesn't have any cancer in Heaven.

Everything from God is good. God is a good God and He only has good things in store for you. Remember that God is NEVER YOUR PROBLEM. So if something bad happens in your life, don't get mad at your good God; get mad at that bad devil!

# Chapter 4
# In The Beginning

In establishing God's will concerning healing, it is also helpful in taking a look at Creation. When God was creating the earth and everything within it, He said it was good. All that God did was good.

*1* In the beginning God created the heavens and the earth. *2* The earth was without form, and void; and darkness was on the face of the deep. And the Spirit of God was hovering over the face of the waters. *3* Then God said, "Let there be light"; and there was light. *4* And God saw the light, that it was good; and God divided the light from the darkness. *5* God called the light Day, and the darkness He called Night. So the evening and the morning were the first day. *6* Then God said, "Let there be a firmament in the midst of the waters, and let it divide the waters from the waters." *7* Thus God made the firmament, and divided the waters which were under the firmament from the waters which were above the firmament; and it was so. *8* And God called the firmament Heaven. So the evening and the morning were the second day. *9* Then God said, "Let the waters under the heavens be gathered together into one place, and let the dry land appear"; and it was so. *10* And God called the dry land Earth, and the gathering together of the waters He called Seas. And God saw that it was good. *11* Then God said, "Let the earth bring forth grass, the herb that yields seed, and the fruit tree that yields fruit according to its kind, whose seed is in itself, on the earth"; and it was so. *12* And the earth brought forth grass, the herb that yields seed according to its kind, and the tree that yields fruit, whose seed is in itself according to its kind. And God saw that it was good. *13* So the evening and the morning were the third day. *14* Then God said, "Let there be lights in the firmament of the heavens to divide the day from the night; and let them be for signs and seasons, and for days and years; *15* and let them be for lights in the firmament of the heavens to give light on the earth"; and it was so. *16* Then God made two great lights: the greater light to rule the day, and the lesser light to rule the night. He made the stars also. *17* God set them in the firmament of the heavens to give light on the earth, *18* and to rule over the day and over the night, and to divide the light from the darkness. And God saw that it was good. *19* So the evening and the morning were the fourth day. *20* Then God said, "Let the waters abound with an abundance of living creatures, and let birds fly above the earth across the face of the firmament of the heavens." *21* So God created great sea creatures and every living thing that moves, with which the waters abounded, according to their kind, and every winged bird according to its kind. And God saw that it was good. *22* And God blessed them, saying, "Be fruitful and multiply, and fill the waters in the seas, and let birds multiply on the earth." *23* So the evening and the morning were the fifth day. *24* Then God said, "Let the earth bring forth the living creature according to its kind: cattle and creeping thing and beast of the earth, each according to its kind"; and it was so. *25* And God made the beast of the earth according to its kind, cattle according to its kind, and everything that creeps on the earth according to its kind. And God saw that it was good. *26* Then God said, "Let Us make man in Our image, according to Our likeness; let them have dominion over the fish of the sea, over the birds of the air, and over the cattle, over all the earth and over every creeping thing that creeps on the earth." *27* So God created man in His own image; in the image of God He created him; male and female He created them. *28* Then God blessed them, and God said to them, "Be fruitful and multiply; fill the earth and subdue it; have dominion over the fish of the sea, over the birds of the air, and over every living thing that moves on the earth." *29* And God said, "See, I have given you every herb that yields seed which is on the face of all the earth, and every tree whose fruit yields seed; to you it shall be for food. *30* Also, to every beast of the earth, to every bird of the air, and to everything that creeps on the earth, in which there is life, I have given every green herb for food"; and it was so. *31* Then God saw everything that He had made, and indeed it was very good. So the evening and the morning were the sixth day.

**Genesis 1:1-31**

I find it interesting that in the entire account of creation, there is no mention of sickness or disease. God made all kinds of stuff, but no sickness. Did you notice God made a tree of life but didn't make a tree of sickness? Even when God made man, He made everything about man good.

**26 Then God said, "Let Us make man in Our image, according to Our likeness; let them have dominion over the fish of the sea, over the birds of the air, and over the cattle, over all the earth and over every creeping thing that creeps on the earth." 27 So God created man in His own image; in the image of God He created him; male and female He created them.**

**Genesis 1:26-27**

Man was made in the image of God. Does God have sickness? No. Is God subject to sickness? No. God didn't make man sick nor did He create sickness and disease and place it in the garden. Everything God made was good; everything He made was perfect.

All that God created was made to induce and sustain life; sickness doesn't sustain life. Sickness does not allow one to be fruitful and multiply. It doesn't take much common sense to figure this out. God didn't make sickness. God didn't make man nor any of His creation to be sick. Everything God wanted in man and in the earth, He made; yet, sickness was not one of them.

In summary, if God's will was for you to be sick, he would have created man with sickness; He would have established man with sickness. If God wanted disease in the earth, He would have created it, but He didn't. God made man free of disease - that is His will!

# Chapter 5
# God's Will In Heaven

*9* In this manner, therefore, pray: Our Father in heaven, Hallowed be Your name. *10* Your kingdom come. Your will be done On earth as it is in heaven.
**Matthew 6:9-10**

In the famous Lord's Prayer, Jesus prayed that God's will in Heaven be done on Earth. Why did He pray that way? Because Heaven is the model. God's original plan was for earth to be like Heaven. In the very beginning, God made Eden perfect and left Adam and Eve in control. God's plan for Adam was to go throughout the rest of the earth and make it like Eden. Unfortunately, because of Adam's sin, he lost his dominion.

Jesus came to restore our dominion. He also came to show us how to have heaven on earth. This is why Jesus prayed in the manner He did - that God's will in heaven would be done on earth.

God put on Earth what was in Heaven. Is there any sickness in Heaven? No! Is there any death in Heaven? No! Are there any crippled people, blind people, or deformed people in Heaven? No! Well, if that isn't God's will in Heaven, then it isn't His will on the Earth. Again, you can see this with creation. God's will in on earth was revealed through creation.  You could also say that God's will in Heaven was also revealed through creation.

Jesus didn't want any sickness on the earth.  Jesus didn't want any disease on the earth.  He didn't want to see people maimed and deformed.  He didn't want to see people not living out their full lives because of sickness and disease. Cancer, pneumonia, arthritis, blindness, deafness and fibromyalgia were not part of Heaven's plan; therefore, they weren't part of earth's plan.  God's plan never included sickness!

Jesus came to carry out God's will on the earth - which was God's will in Heaven.  In one sense, you could say it like this, "Father, your health be done on earth as it is in heaven!"

# Chapter 6
# The Origin of Sickness

So where did sickness originate from? That's easy. Before Adam sinned, he was the god of the earth, but when Adam sinned and turned his authority over to Satan, he died spiritually. Satan took control, the earth became cursed and death began to reign and rule.

> *17* Then to Adam He said, "Because you have heeded the voice of your wife, and have eaten from the tree of which I commanded you, saying, 'You shall not eat of it': "Cursed is the ground for your sake; In toil you shall eat of it All the days of your life. *18* Both thorns and thistles it shall bring forth for you, And you shall eat the herb of the field. *19* In the sweat of your face you shall eat bread Till you return to the ground, For out of it you were taken; For dust you are, And to dust you shall return."
>
> **Genesis 3:17-19**

The earth became cursed. Through the curse came sickness, disease, poverty, lack, etc. God didn't create bad things; Satan just took away what was good and the automatic result was bad.

> *4* In Him was life and the life was the light of men.
>
> **John 1:4**

If you want darkness, just turn out the light. That is what happened in the very beginning. The light of blessing was turned off and the result was the darkness of the curse. Adam was the light in the world; he was full of God who is light. Dominion over the earth was placed in his hands, but he voluntarily turned his light off forever changing the course of history. His light was turned out and the curse exploded in the earth ravaging everything. Now, Satan was in control as was the curse.

> **10 The thief comes only to steal and kill and destroy; I have come that they may have life, and have it to the full.**
>
> **John 10:10 NIV**

Where health ruled, sickness now reigned supreme. Where more than enough ruled, now lack reigned supreme. None of this was God's fault. God set up the earth to be a place of nothing missing, nothing broken. That is what the blessing of God was all about! The blessing of God was life, health, peace and prosperity! Take the blessing away and you are left with death, sickness, anxiety and lack.

So, you can't blame God for any of this mess on the earth. He made the earth perfect and Adam messed it up. The origin of sickness and disease is the result of the curse that came upon the earth through Adam's sin.

# Chapter 7
# Old Testament Symbols

In the Christian world, many times you hear about types and shadows in the Old Testament. What they are referring to are figures, events, or things which were, in a sense, a foreshadowing of things to come. For example, Joshua, who led the Israelites into the Promised Land, is often considered a type of Jesus. First of all, the name Joshua can also be translated as Jesus. Secondly, Joshua led God's people, the Israelites, into the Promised Land; this is what Jesus did for us through His death, burial and resurrection. Joshua was a temporal savior; Christ is our spiritual Savior.

In regards to healing, there are many types and shadows, but I am going to focus on two in particular which I believe are the easiest to see and will be the most beneficial to you.

## The Bronze Serpent

The first symbol we are going to look at is the bronze serpent found in Numbers 21. During the time the Israelites were wandering through the desert, there was one particular instance where they were attacked by the Canaanites and several Israelites were taken prisoner. Israel prayed to God for deliverance from the enemy; as a result, God heard their prayer and gave them total victory. The Bible says that the Israelites "utterly destroyed them and their cities."

After a great victory, it wasn't long before the Israelites began griping at God again. (If you read of the Israelites journey through the wilderness, you will find that their bickering and complaining was an all too common occurrence!) Tired, thirsty, and hungry, they decided to take out their frustrations on God and Moses.

When this happened, venomous snakes came into the Israelite camp and began biting the people which caused many deaths. So, when the Israelites realized the consequence of their sin, they admitted their wrong to Moses and begged him to pray that God would take away the snakes. When Moses prayed, this was God's response:

> **8 Then the LORD said to Moses, "Make a fiery serpent, and set it on a pole; and it shall be that everyone who is bitten, when he looks at it, shall live." 9 So Moses made a bronze serpent, and put it on a pole; and so it was, if a serpent had bitten anyone, when he looked at the bronze serpent, he lived.**
>
> **Numbers 21:8-9**

Do you see how that symbolized Jesus? Well, let me make it very clear for you. Do you know John 3:16?

> **16 For God so loved the world that He gave His only begotten Son, that whoever believes in Him should not perish but have everlasting life.**
>
> **John 3:16**

Most people know John 3:16, but have you ever read a few of the preceding verses? In John 3, Jesus was talking to Nicodemus who was one of the leading religious figures of that day. Jesus was explaining the need for salvation and then made these statements:

> *14* And as Moses lifted up the serpent in the wilderness, even so must the Son of Man be lifted up, *15* that whoever believes in Him should not perish but have eternal life. *16* For God so loved the world that He gave His only begotten Son, that whoever believes in Him should not perish but have everlasting life. *17* For God did not send His Son into the world to condemn the world, but that the world through Him might be saved.
>
> **John 3:14-17**

Notice what Jesus said in verse 14: "And as Moses lifted up the serpent in the wilderness, so must the Son of Man be lifted up." The bronze snake was a type of Jesus on the cross. The bronze snake represented not only safety, but also healing for the Israelites. Jesus did not represent salvation and healing - *He is salvation and healing.* The bronze snake was a symbol; Jesus was the real deal!

My purpose for showing this to you is for one simple reason: healing is God's idea! It is a major theme running throughout the entire Bible. God provided healing in the Old Testament and He provided healing in the New Testament. If a shadow or type of Christ could heal someone, how much more so the actual Christ heal us of all sickness and disease?

## The Passover Lamb

Let's take a look at another type of Jesus found in the Old Testament. In Exodus 12, we find God's instructions to the

Israelites about the Passover Lamb.

> 5 The animals you choose must be year-old males without defect, and you may take them from the sheep or the goats. 6 Take care of them until the fourteenth day of the month, when all the people of the community of Israel must slaughter them at twilight. 7 Then they are to take some of the blood and put it on the sides and tops of the doorframes of the houses where they eat the lambs. 8 That same night they are to eat the meat roasted over the fire, along with bitter herbs, and bread made without yeast. 9 Do not eat the meat raw or cooked in water, but roast it over the fire--head, legs and inner parts. 10 Do not leave any of it till morning; if some is left till morning, you must burn it. 11 This is how you are to eat it: with your cloak tucked into your belt, your sandals on your feet and your staff in your hand. Eat it in haste; it is the Lord's Passover. 12 "On that same night I will pass through Egypt and strike down every firstborn-- both men and animals--and I will bring judgment on all the gods of Egypt. I am the Lord. 13 The blood will be a sign for you on the houses where you are; and when I see the blood, I will pass over you. No destructive plague will touch you when I strike Egypt."
>
> **Exodus 12:5-13 NIV**

Notice what God said in verse 13, "No destructive plague will touch you." Praise God!  No plague, no sickness, no disease would touch them because they partook of the Passover lamb and put the blood over their door.

You see, the Passover lamb is a type of Jesus as well. The blood and body of Christ was sacrificed for the forgiveness of our sin and the healing of our bodies. Just as the blood was applied to the Israelites' doors, the blood of Christ was applied to our hearts and cleansed us from all sin, all sickness, and all disease. Take a look at what Paul said in 1 Corinthians 5:7.

> **7 Therefore purge out the old leaven, that you may be a new lump, since you truly are unleavened. For indeed Christ, our Passover, was sacrificed for us.**
>
> **1 Corinthians 5:7**

Christ was our Passover Lamb. There are several times when Jesus is referred to as the Lamb of God, such as when John the Baptist saw Jesus approaching him to be baptized.

> **29 The next day John saw Jesus coming toward him, and said, "Behold! The Lamb of God who takes away the sin of the world!**
>
> **John 1:29**

If the shadow of the real could bring healing to God's people, how much more so the real thing bring healing? If a little lamb could bring healing, how much more so The Lamb of God?

God provided healing for the Israelites through types and shadows of the coming Christ. Then, through Christ's death, burial and resurrection, God provided healing once and for all - for all people. God provided healing under the Old Testament and under the New Testament. Why? Because God's will is for you to be healed!

# Chapter 8
# God's First A.K.A.

If you have watched just a small portion of television, you have heard of the many entertainers and their a.k.a.'s (also known as). Some of these are nicknames that have just stuck with them over the years and some are names the person themselves have picked out.

One person who really stands out when it comes to a.k.a.'s is professional basketball player Shaquille O'Neil. Shaquille is famous for his self-imposed names such as, The Diesel, The Big Aristotle, The Big Felon, The Big Cordially and Shaq-Fu. Even though these names are silly, they identify some sort of characteristic about Shaq and the way he plays basketball. Even though Shaq has come up with a long list of a.k.a.'s, he isn't the first one to do so.

Did you know the first a.k.a wasn't for a human being? The first a.k.a was given by God; God gave Himself an a.k.a. There are several names attributed to God by individuals and many that God gave Himself. Like many individuals, God gave Himself a.k.a.'s to reveal different characteristics of His personality and nature.

In light of our study, it is very interesting to note the first a.k.a God gave Himself in order to reveal Himself to humanity. The first name God gave Himself was JEHOVAH ROPHE, "The Lord Who Heals."

**26** He said, "If you listen carefully to the voice of the Lord your God and do what is right in his eyes, if you pay attention to his commands and keep all his decrees, I will not bring on you (allow) any of the diseases I brought on the Egyptians, for I am the Lord, who heals you."

**Exodus 15:26 NIV**
**Parenthesis are author's note**

God could have revealed so many things about Himself to the Israelites, but He chose first and foremost to reveal Himself as the Healer.  He saved the Israelites from their enemies and then began speaking to them about healing.  Isn't it wonderful to know that God is the Healer?

Although, theologians all over the world say that according to this scripture, God puts sickness on people.  You have to understand that again, the translators made a mistake.  With the Hebrew language, they had a choice to translate the verb in either a causative tense or permissive tense; they chose wrong and went with causative.  God didn't send all the plagues.  Satan sent the plagues; God allowed it because of judgement.

The Hebrew language isn't as big as our English language, so sometimes the translators had a bit more difficulty.  Yet, if you interpret the Old Testament in light of the New Testament, you will never go wrong.

You see, if you read Exodus 15:26 in light of John 10:10 and Acts 10:38, it would definitely help you in your understanding.  Unfortunately, many people do not interpret scripture with the rest of the Bible.  They take one scripture out of context and say it isn't God will to heal.  How can someone look at

God's first redemptive name and still believe God isn't the Healer?

I am the Lord Your Healer. How much more plain and simple does it get? *God is saying He is the Healer and people are saying God isn't it.* Who is right? Well, seeing that God is God and He has never made a mistake...hmm...I think I will choose God.

Throughout the Bible, God reveals Himself as, The Lord Our Righteousness, The Lord Our Peace, The Lord Our Banner, The Lord Who Sanctifies and the list goes on and on. Why didn't God reveal any of these other names before revealing that He is the Healer? Because all these other things are great, but if you are sick, you could care less about anything else.

When you get down to the nitty-gritty, human beings have three basic needs: shelter, food, and health. When you don't have one of those, you could care less about anything else in life. If you haven't eaten in three days, do you think you will be concerned about seeing the latest movie? No way! The only thing on your mind will be food.

If you are sick and diseased, will you really care if God tells you He is your Righteousness? I know this sounds bad, but, honestly, most people won't because the average Christian doesn't understand that healing is included in righteousness. What shows a sick person that you love them the most: (a) heal them, or (b) tell them they are righteous?

You see, the Israelites were just getting to know God; they didn't know much about Him. If they were to follow God and trust Him with their lives, He had to show them He would take care of them. God had to reveal that He had their best interests at heart. He had to reveal to the Israelites that first and foremost, their basic needs would be met.

Seriously think about this. If someone is hungry, they aren't going to listen to you. If someone has a high fever and can't keep their food down, many times what you say to them will go in one ear and out the other. Why? Nothing else matters until basic needs are met. Even animals understand this! If you want to gain the trust of a stray animal, give them some food and shelter - meet their basic needs and they will begin to trust you.

God had just brought the Israelites out into the wilderness. They had been slaves for hundreds of years; all they knew was Egypt and the ways of Egypt. Now, they were in the middle of nowhere following Moses, whom they really didn't know and following God whom they had no clue about.

God loved them so much that He saved them and then told them not to every worry about getting sick. For the rest of their lives, they had the Doctor of all Doctors at their disposal! But get this: God doesn't change; He is still the same yesterday, today and forever.

> *17* **Whatever is good and perfect comes down to us from God our Father, who created all the lights in the heavens. He never changes or casts a shifting shadow.**
>
> **James 1:17 NLT**

If God was the Healer back then, He is most certainly the Healer today. If God was the Healer for His servants, He is most certainly the Healer for His children. Later on, we will see that God continued these actions with Jesus. Jesus preached salvation and preached healing. When Jesus gave the great commission, He sent the disciples on a mission to bring salvation and healing to the world!

Praise God! God is the Healer! God is my Healer! God is your Healer! For all those who say God's will is not to heal, check up on God's first a.k.a.: JEHOVAH ROPHE - The Lord Who Heals!

# Chapter 9
# Rich, Healthy Job

Poor old Job. Hasn't the world heard that phrase long enough? Well, I have. Job wasn't poor. Job went through a little storm of life. He was hit pretty hard in his finances and his health, but he came out of it; although, listening to most people, you would think Job's entire life was misery and sorrow.

Actually, I think too many people use the story of Job as a crutch. They are miserable, their marriage is miserable, their home is miserable, their health is miserable, even the cockroaches in their house are miserable. People use Job's story to justify their miserable lives.

Well, sniff, sniff, whah, whah. Read your Bible! Pull the pacifier out of your mouth, take the pampers off your butt, wipe your eyes, blow your nose and start living the victorious life God created for you! If you want to use Job as an example, then focus on being as rich as he was and then turn around and be a blessing to the world!

The story of Job is probably the most misunderstood book of the Bible. Due to Job's story, people have thought it isn't God's will for people to be healed, that God is a mean God, and that God sends catastrophe's on people. The book of Job is usually misunderstood due to two reasons: (1) people haven't read the whole book (2) people haven't read the book of Job in light of the New Testament. Let's take a brief look at his story beginning with the first chapter of Job.

> *1* There was a man in the land of Uz, whose name was Job; and that man was blameless and upright, and one who feared God and shunned evil.   *2* And seven sons and three daughters were born to him.   *3* Also, his possessions were seven thousand sheep, three thousand camels, five hundred yoke of oxen, five hundred female donkeys, and a very large household, so that this man was the greatest of all the people of the East.   *9* Does Job fear God for nothing?" Satan replied.   *10* "Have you not put a hedge around him and his household and everything he has? You have blessed the work of his hands, so that his flocks and herds are spread throughout the land."
>
> Job 1:1-3, 9-10

First of all, I want you to notice that Job was blessed.  He was the richest man in the entire Eastern world!  Even Satan understood that God had protected Job and his family from poverty, sickness, and destruction.

Job was protected and prosperous because of God's blessing on his life.  You see, before the "suffering" of Job, this man was living large!  Although, understand that Job's famous suffering came because of something Job did - not because of God.

> *1* There once was a man named Job who lived in the land of Uz. He was blameless—a man of complete integrity. He feared God and stayed away from evil. *2* He had seven sons and three daughters. *3* He owned 7,000 sheep, 3,000 camels, 500 teams of oxen, and 500 female donkeys. He also had many servants. He was, in fact, the richest person in that

entire area. *4* Job's sons would take turns preparing feasts in their homes, and they would also invite their three sisters to celebrate with them. *5* When these celebrations ended—sometimes after several days—Job would purify his children. He would get up early in the morning and offer a burnt offering for each of them. For Job said to himself, "Perhaps my children have sinned and have cursed God in their hearts." This was Job's regular practice.

**Job 1:1-5  NLT**

Did you notice what Job was doing?  He was so concerned that his children were sinning, he was constantly offering sacrifices.  In other  words, Job was scared for his children; he wasn't living in faith -  Job was living in fear.  When you operate in faith, you open the door for God; when you operate in fear, you open the door for Satan.

*6* One day the angels came to present themselves before the Lord, and Satan also came with them. *7* The Lord said to Satan, "Where have you come from?" Satan answered the Lord, "From roaming through the earth and going back and forth in it." *8* Then the Lord said to Satan, "Have you considered my servant Job? There is no one on earth like him; he is blameless and upright, a man who fears God and shuns evil." *9* "Does Job fear God for nothing?" Satan replied. *10* "Have you not put a hedge around him and his household and everything he has? You have blessed the work of his hands, so that his flocks and herds are spread throughout the land. *11* But stretch out your hand and strike everything he has, and he will surely curse you to your face." *12* **The Lord said to Satan, "Very well, then, everything he has is in your hands, but on the man himself do not lay a finger." Then Satan went out from the presence of the Lord.**

Job 1:6-12

Because of Job's fear, he had placed himself outside the blessing. Job himself had stepped outside God's protection; this is why God told Satan in verse 12 that everything Job had was in Satan's hands.

It is just like a person using an umbrella. As long as they stay under the umbrella, they stay dry; yet, when they step outside of the umbrella's protection, they get wet.

God is holding His umbrella of protection over each and every one of us. As long as we stay in faith and stay in His will, we stay under the umbrella. But when we get into fear, we step out from under the umbrella.

Now is it your fault or God's fault when you get wet? It is most assuredly yours! Why? Because you chose to step out from under the umbrella! This same situation occurs each and every day all over the world. Something bad happens to someone and they blame God; yet, they don't take a step back and wonder, "Hmm, I wonder if it could have been my fault?" Why is it we never think, "Could I be the problem?" After all, God never makes mistakes!

You have to understand that the calamities in Job's life were not the result of God; it was the result of Job's fear. Yet, all over the world, people blame God for poor old Job's suffering. They say God killed his family, God took away Job's stuff and God made him extremely sick.

Remember what I said about reading the story of Job in line with the rest of the Bible?  Remember what I said earlier?  God good...devil bad!  What does John 10:10 say?  God gives life; Satan kills, steals and destroys.

God is never to blame!  Never!  Yet, somehow all those who think God did all the bad things to Job seem to skip over this verse:

> **6 And the Lord said to Satan, "Behold, he is in your hand, but spare his life." 7 So Satan went out from the presence of the Lord, and struck Job with painful boils from the sole of his foot to the crown of his head.**
>
> **Job 2:6-7**

Whoa!  Wait a minute! Who struck Job with the painful boils?  Notice, it was Satan who went and struck Job with boils; it was not God.  God is a good God and He doesn't make people sick.  Was it God's will for Job to be sick?  By all means no; yet, because God is a just God and has given us a free will, He will allow us to do and say anything we want.  Job was wrong in being fearful and because of Job's decision, Job allowed Satan free access into his life.

You see, when Job stepped into fear, he stepped into Satan's territory.  When you are in faith, everything you have is in God's hands; when you are in fear, everything you have is in Satan's hands.  It doesn't matter if it's your finances, family, health, house, cars, etc; Satan wants to take away everything you have!

> *25 For the thing I greatly feared has come upon me, And what I dreaded has happened to me. 26 I*

am not at ease, nor am I quiet; I have no rest, for trouble comes.

Job 3:25-26

Job's statement in verse 25 tells you exactly why everything happened.  Job was in fear! Job wasn't trusting God!  (For a deeper understanding on the subject of fear, please read Chad's book entitled *Fearless*.)

Another part of Job's story most people fail to read is the very last chapter of Job.  Job finally realized that he was wrong.  In Job 42:3, Job told God, "Therefore, I have uttered what I did not understand."  Job got things right before God and look at what happened to "poor old Job."

> **10 And the Lord restored Job's losses when he prayed for his friends. Indeed the Lord gave Job twice as much as he had before. 11 Then all his brothers, all his sisters, and all those who had been his acquaintances before, came to him and ate food with him in his house; and they consoled him and comforted him for all the adversity that the Lord had brought upon him. Each one gave him a piece of silver and each a ring of gold. 12 Now the Lord blessed the latter days of Job more than his beginning; for he had fourteen thousand sheep, six thousand camels, one thousand yoke of oxen, and one thousand female donkeys. 13 He also had seven sons and three daughters. 14 And he called the name of the first Jemimah, the name of the second Keziah, and the name of the third Keren-Happuch. 15 In all the land were found no women so beautiful as the daughters of Job; and their father gave them an inheritance among their**

brothers. *16* After this Job lived one hundred and forty years, and saw his children and grandchildren for four generations. *17* So Job died, old and full of days.

**Job 42:10-17**

There are a few key things I want you to see in this. Number one, verse 10 says that God gave Job twice as much as he had before. Understand this please! God wants to prosper you, not take away your stuff. God is a giver, Satan is a taker. Contrary to what Job said in Job 1:21, God does not give and take away! Job said that in ignorance and was flat out wrong in his statement.

There is a popular Christian song played on the radio and sung in churches all over the world that represents this lie from the pit of hell. The verse says, "He gives and takes away, He gives and takes away. Our hearts will choose to say, blessed be His name." If that isn't the worst indictment against God I've ever heard, I don't know what is. God isn't a taker; God is a giver!

If you are singing that song, STOP! When I or Lacy hear it on the radio, the radio is immediately turned off. If it is on your ipod, ipad, mp3 player, whatever your listening device - delete it. If you listen to false doctrine, you'll start believing false doctrine. Just because it's on Christian radio or Christian television doesn't mean that it is true.

Now, lets take a look at verse 12. The second point I want you to see in Job's story is that God blessed the latter days of Job more than the beginning!

> *12* Now the Lord blessed the latter days of Job more than his beginning; for he had fourteen thousand sheep, six thousand camels, one thousand yoke of oxen, and one thousand female donkeys.
>
> **Job 42:12**

Praise God! Yep, sure looks like Job's life was just terrible. Most of these people preaching about Job and his suffering need to shut up and read the whole story.

Job spent around 9 months doing a little self-induced suffering and spent the rest of his life in some God-induced prospering! Praise God! He was a healthy rich man before and a healthier, richer man afterward! God is so good!

> *16* After this Job lived one hundred and forty years, and saw his children and grandchildren for four generations. *17* So Job died, old and full of days.
>
> **Job 42:16-17**

Oh I love it! Job lived to be one hundred forty years old. That was one healthy and rich old man! The Bible says that Job died old and full of days; he died with his health and he left his children one mammoth inheritance.

Although, listen to most ignorant preachers talk about Job and it is a story of heartache, misery, and an all out attack on how, supposedly, God just sometimes decides to punish His people. That is just a bunch of garbage!

God's will for Job was that of prosperity in every area of his life, including Job's health.  Because Job got into fear, he lost everything, but when Job realized his mistake, he got back in faith, stepped back into God's protection - and this dude got overwhelmed with the blessing of God!  Understand this and understand it well: God isn't out to get you; He is out to get things to you!  One of those things is health for your body!

# Chapter 10

# Is Healing For All Or Just For Some?

Is it God's will to heal me? That is a common question that runs through everyone's mind at some point in their life. You see some people receive their healing and wonder if they were just one of the "lucky ones." Does God provide healing for certain people and not you?

This is one issue that has to be answered with certainty in order for you to have faith for healing. Remember, faith begins where the will of God is known. I want you to know, beyond a shadow of a doubt that God desires to see you healed of all sickness and disease.

> *17* **For the Lord your God is God of gods and Lord of lords, the great God, mighty and awesome, who shows no partiality and accepts no bribes.**
> **Deuteronomy 10:17**

> *11* **For God does not show favoritism.**
> **Romans 2:11 NLT**

> 6 **But from those who seemed to be something-- whatever they were, it makes no difference to me; God shows personal favoritism to no man--for those who seemed to be something added nothing to me.**
> **Galatians 2:6**

God doesn't have favorites.  He doesn't care if you are black or white, poor or rich, tall or short, American or French, Christian or Muslim - God wants all people healed.  For God to offer something to one person and not to another would go against the very nature and character of God.

Did God show favoritism with salvation?  Certainly not.  I never have seen in my Bible where God told Jesus salvation was only for a select few.

> **13 For "Everyone who calls on the name of the LORD will be saved."**
>
> **Romans 10:13  NLT**

Most people pretty much accept the truth that God's will is for everyone to be saved; although, that is not widely accepted view regarding healing.  The problem with that is this: I have also never seen anywhere in my Bible where Jesus turned someone down for healing.

My point is, if He did it for one, He will do it for you!  God doesn't play favorites!  If God saved one, He will save you.  If God healed one, He will heal you.  God's absolute will is to see you healed and whole!

There is something else I want to point out to you.  Did you ever notice that all the people healed in the Bible were sinners?  All the healings mentioned in the Old Testament - they were all sinners who received healing!  All the people who received healing under Jesus' ministry - they were all sinners.  You see, no one could be a Christian until Jesus died, rose again and sat down at the right hand of God.

Does it make sense that God would heal those that were

sinners, but not heal those who had been saved by the precious blood of Jesus? *Would God provide healing for sinners, but keep the saints sick?* That just doesn't make sense! If He healed those under the Old Covenant, how much greater is His desire to heal those under the New Covenant?

Again, if God healed one, He will heal you. God's will is that all people be free of sickness and disease just as much as it is His will for all to be saved. You would be hard pressed to find many church going people who do not believe salvation is for all; although, ask them if healing is for all and you will get all sorts of hee-haw answers.

So let's get this issue taken care of right now. God wants all people healed. If we can establish this truth, then we can know with all certainty God wants you healed. "All" means "all" doesn't it? Let's look at some instances of healing in the ministry of Jesus.

> **23 And Jesus went about all Galilee, teaching in their synagogues, preaching the gospel of the kingdom, and healing all kinds of sickness and all kinds of disease among the people. 24 Then His fame went throughout all Syria; and they brought to Him all sick people who were afflicted with various diseases and torments, and those who were demon-possessed, epileptics, and paralytics; and He healed them.**
>
> **Matthew 4:23-24**

Everyone that was brought to Jesus was healed. Isn't that wonderful? Jesus did not care what kind of sickness or disease they had; He did not even care who they were! As long as they believed, Jesus healed them.

> **35** Then Jesus went about all the cities and villages, teaching in their synagogues, preaching the gospel of the kingdom, and healing every sickness and every disease among the people.
>
> Matthew 9:35

Again, we see no favoritism among people or types of sickness. Come one, come all! Jesus healed every sickness and every disease among the people. You see, no disease is too big for God. Stage 4 cancer - that isn't anything for my big God! Fibromyalgia, anemia, lung cancer, brain tumors, and multiple sclerosis are nothing for God. In God's eyes, a brain tumor is the same as a wart on your finger.

I have literally seen and felt cancerous tumors the size of a golf ball dissolve under my hand. It wasn't me who healed that person; it was the big God on the inside of me who kills cancer! Because I am one with Christ and He is one with me, I can kill cancer too! Glory to God! God can take care of anything if you will only believe!

> **15** But when Jesus knew it, He withdrew from there. And great multitudes followed Him, and He healed them all.
>
> Matthew 12:15

This is turning into a common theme, "and He healed them all." Jesus healed them all. Everyone who came in faith for healing received their healing regardless of background, lifestyle, age, race, and ethnicity.

Do you realize that God will even heal someone that is not of your denomination? Yes He will. He will even heal someone that is a Buddhist, Atheist, Hindu or Muslim. Pick your jaw off the ground because it is true.  He will heal a sinner; believe me, it is in the Bible and I have personally see it many times in my ministry as well.

Many times He will meet the need of that individual to show that He is the One true God and reveal His unending love for them.  If you are a person, God wants you healed!

> *13* When Jesus heard it, He departed from there by boat to a deserted place by Himself. But when the multitudes heard it, they followed Him on foot from the cities. *14* And when Jesus went out He saw a great multitude; and He was moved with compassion for them, and healed their sick.
>
> Matthew 14:13-14

Jesus was moved with compassion and healed all their sick. He healed multitudes of people!  You are talking about thousands upon thousands of people...and every sick person was healed.  Why did He heal them?  He loved them!  Why does God want you healed?  He loves you!  God loves you more than you love yourself!  *God wants you healed more than you want to be healed!*

> *34* When they had crossed over, they came to the land of Gennesaret. *35* And when the men of that place recognized Him, they sent out into all that surrounding region, brought to Him all who were sick, *36* and begged Him that they might only touch the hem of His garment. And as many as touched it were made perfectly well.
>
> Matthew 14:34-36

I hope you are seeing this by now. Anyone that was sick and came to Jesus for healing - they got it. All the sick were brought to Him and all those who touched His garment were made well. Did you notice that Jesus didn't make them somewhat well, half well or even three-quarters well? He made them perfectly well! God will drive all sickness and disease from your body. He doesn't allow any of it to stay; the power of God sends all sickness packing.

Sickness and disease can't stay at your place anymore! After all, your body is the temple of God, the dwelling place of God. God doesn't want His house full of pests!

> **17 And He came down with them and stood on a level place with a crowd of His disciples and a great multitude of people from all Judea and Jerusalem, and from the seacoast of Tyre and Sidon, who came to hear Him and be healed of their diseases, 18 as well as those who were tormented with unclean spirits. And they were healed. 19 And the whole multitude sought to touch Him, for power went out from Him and healed them all.**
>
> **Luke 6:17-18**

This may seem a little repetitive, but I want you to see all these instances of people coming to Jesus and all being healed. Why? If He would heal them, He will heal you. If you are a person, you are an "all." This was a great multitude, untold thousands of people, and all the sick were healed. Healing is for everyone, not just a select few.

I have one more scripture for you to show you along these lines. This is one of my favorite scriptures and one you need to have etched into your mind!

**38 How God anointed Jesus of Nazareth with the Holy Spirit and with power, who went about doing good and healing all who were oppressed by the devil, for God was with Him.**

**Acts 10:38**

This is one of the things Jesus was sent to do: heal all those who were oppressed by the devil. Who was doing the oppressing? That stupid devil! Who was putting sickness on people? Yep, that stupid devil again! Remember, God good; devil bad. Everywhere there was sickness - God was ready to wipe it out. Healing for every sickness; healing for every disease; healing for every person!

God loves you and He wants you healed and whole. If He healed one, He will heal you. It is His will! It is His desire to see you well. I just showed you six instances where everyone who came to Jesus for healing received it.

He didn't turn one person away. You will never find one person in the Bible who came to God for healing in which it was not God's will to heal them. You will never find one instance in Jesus' earthly ministry where He turned someone down for healing. Healing is for you!

# Chapter 11

# If It Isn't God's Will To Heal All

There are not too many Biblical topics which have caused more confusion and division more so than "God's will concerning healing." Unlearned, hard-hearted, ignorant men have taken simple Bible truths and have conformed those truths to fit their lives and personal experiences instead of conforming their lives to the simple Bible truths.

The Bible is simple, but goofy men have gone and placed their own interpretation on the Bible instead of allowing the Bible to interpret itself. If you read enough scripture in context concerning a particular topic, you will always find the perfect, complete and Godly answer.

In the case of God's will concerning healing, if one was to look up every scripture concerning healing, they would never find one scripture stating that God's will is not to heal everyone. They would never find God nor Jesus turning someone away that needed healing. They would be hard pressed to find any evidence that would support their belief that God will not heal everyone that comes to Him in faith.

Concerning healing, if a man was to tell me that God's will is not to heal everyone, I would most assuredly conclude at least one of three things (a) this man does not know God experientially (b) he is basing his belief on life experiences (c) he is taking a scripture out of context.

God has given us so much scripture revealing that it is His will to heal everyone that a man would have to possess Jello for a brain to look at all of them and still think God doesn't want everyone healed.

Below is a list of twelve things to ponder regarding the topic of God's will concerning healing. These are just simple, common sense questions that you must ask if someone believes it isn't God's will to heal everyone. I simply want you to think about each statement/question and ponder the absurdity and yet seriousness of it.  If it isn't God's will to heal everyone, then these are all legitimate questions that must be asked and answered.

1. If it isn't God's will to heal everyone, then Jesus failed to fulfill His mission on the earth and the prophet Isaiah was a false prophet.

2. If it isn't God's will to heal everyone, then how can one have faith to be healed since Jesus told people it was their faith that brought their healing?

3. If it isn't God's will to heal everyone, then almost every Greek and Hebrew scholar has failed in their interpretation of the word *salvation*.

4. If it isn't God's will to heal everyone, then God is a respecter of persons; therefore He is a liar; therefore, He isn't God because the Bible says that God is truth; therefore, since the world is upheld by His Word and His Word is no good, then we can no longer exist.

5. If it isn't God's will to heal everyone, then Jesus went

against God's will and therefore was a sinner because everywhere He went, Jesus healed ALL that came to Him.

6. If it isn't God's will to heal everyone, then every person in the medical profession is against God and has more compassion than God because they endeavor to help every sick and diseased person to become whole again.

7. If it isn't God's will to heal everyone, then every person in the medical profession is in sin because they are going against God's will.

8. If it isn't God's will to heal every Christian, then we should ask God to scrap Christianity and allow us to start living under the Old Covenant as a Jew.

9. If it isn't God's will to heal everyone, then all the parents of the earth love their children more than God loves His own.

10. If it isn't God's will to heal everyone, then God must have been joking when He said He would satisfy us with long life.

11. If it isn't God's will to heal everyone, how would one know if they are one of the fortunate one's for which it is God's will to heal them?

12. If it isn't God's will to heal everyone, then why does every human body instinctively fight sickness, disease, and death? Did not God create the human body?

# Chapter 12
# The Salvation Package

Salvation - now that has been a tremendously misunderstood word. When most Christians think about the word salvation, they automatically think about going to Heaven. Praise God for a ticket to Heaven, but do you realize there is more to salvation than that?

The Hebrew and Greek words for *salvation* imply deliverance, preservation, safety, healing, prosperity and victory. You see, when you receive salvation, you receive more than just a ticket to Heaven; you receive an entire package.

There a number of scriptures throughout the Bible that talk about what I like to call the salvation package; these particular scriptures are usually referred to as the redemption scriptures.

> *4* **Surely He has borne our griefs And carried our sorrows; Yet we esteemed Him stricken, Smitten by God, and afflicted.** *5* **But He was wounded for our transgressions, He was bruised for our iniquities; The chastisement for our peace was upon Him, And by His stripes we are healed.**
>
> **Isaiah 53:4-5**

This passage of scripture is referring to Jesus and the sacrifice He made for us. Because of the translation to English, it is a little difficult for us to grasp the wonderful truths of this passage. There are a few words here that if we look up the Hebrew definition, it definitely opens our eyes to what Jesus really did for us on the cross.

Let us begin with the word *borne*. *Borne* literally means "removed." The words *griefs* and *sorrows* literally mean "sicknesses" and "pains," respectively. So you could read verse four this way: "Surely He has removed our sicknesses and carried our pains."

This passage of scripture is talking about Jesus bearing our sicknesses and diseases. In verse five, the word *iniquities* literally means "weaknesses."

So Jesus not only died for our sins, but He also died for our sicknesses, pains, and weaknesses. The last phrase of verse five makes it very plain: "...And by Whose stripes we are healed." Let's take a look at some other translations that actually translated these words correctly.

> **4 In fact, it was our diseases he bore, our pains from which he suffered; yet we regarded him as punished, stricken and afflicted by God. 5 But he was wounded because of our crimes, crushed because of our sins; the disciplining that makes us whole fell on him, and by his bruises we are healed.**
>
> **Isaiah 53:4-5  CJB**

> **4 Surely our sicknesses he hath borne, And our pains -- he hath carried them, And we -- we have esteemed him plagued, Smitten of God, and afflicted. 5 And he is pierced for our transgressions, Bruised for our iniquities, The chastisement of**

our peace [is] on him, And by his bruise there is healing to us.

**Isaiah 53:4-5 YLT**

When Jesus died for our sins, He also died for our sicknesses. You will notice that in all of the redemption scriptures, there is a common theme:  salvation from sin and salvation from sickness. *There is no true salvation without healing.*

Many people throughout the world claim that Jesus died for our sins, but not for our sicknesses or that He died for our sicknesses, but only for when we get to Heaven.  These claims are not based on the Bible; they are usually based on experiences.  We are not to base our beliefs on what we see, hear, feel or experience; we are to base our beliefs on the Word of God!

> *16* When evening had come, they brought to Him many who were demon-possessed. And He cast out the spirits with a word, and healed all who were sick, *17* that it might be fulfilled which was spoken by Isaiah the prophet, saying: "He Himself took our infirmities And bore our sicknesses."
>
> **Matthew 8:16-17**

In this passage of scripture, Matthew is referring to what the prophet Isaiah had stated; Jesus died not only for our sins, but also our sicknesses.

> *24* Who Himself bore our sins in His own body on the tree, that we, having died to sins, might live for righteousness--by whose stripes you were healed.
>
> **1 Peter 2:24**

Again, we find another disciple, Peter, quoting Isaiah. Notice in both passages of scripture, Matthew and Peter bring out that through the sacrifice of Jesus, our sins and sicknesses were wiped out. Every sin that we would commit and every sickness that would come against us, Jesus bore on the cross.

I would think that if anyone understood what salvation was really about, the disciples would have it down. They spent more than three years with Jesus and even after Jesus arose from the dead, they had other encounters with Him for forty days. They understood salvation wasn't just about going to Heaven; it was about having Heaven on Earth! No sickness in Heaven; no sickness on Earth! Jesus died and rose again so we could have an abundant life now!

> *1* A Psalm of David. Bless the Lord, O my soul; And all that is within me, bless His holy name! *2* Bless the Lord, O my soul, And forget not all His benefits: *3* Who forgives all your iniquities, Who heals all your diseases, *4* Who redeems your life from destruction, Who crowns you with lovingkindness and tender mercies, *5* Who satisfies your mouth with good things, So that your youth is renewed like the eagle's.
>
> Psalm 103:1-5

Apparently, even King David understood about the salvation package. Did you notice what he said in verse 3? "Who forgives all your iniquities and Who heals all your diseases." Again, where you find the forgiveness of sins, you find the healing of sickness.

When you receive salvation, you not only receive the forgiveness of all sins, you also receive the healing of all sickness. It is a package deal. In order to take healing out of the Bible, you have to get rid of salvation; you can't have one without the other. *If healing isn't for today, salvation isn't for today.*

A very familiar story in the Bible is the Israelites crossing the Red Sea. The crossing of the Red Sea is a type of salvation. The Israelites were saved from the hands of their enemy and placed into the hands of God.

> **26 and said, "If you diligently heed the voice of the Lord your God and do what is right in His sight, give ear to His commandments and keep all His statutes, I will put (allow) none of the diseases on you which I have brought (allowed) on the Egyptians. For I am the Lord who heals you."**
>
> **Exodus 15:26**
> **Parentheses are author's note**

Immediately following their salvation from Egypt, God begins to talk to them about healing. At this point in time, the Israelites didn't know much about God. During their time of captivity, their understanding of God had dwindled and they had gotten caught up in the religions of Egypt.

I find it extremely interesting that the first thing God revealed to the Israelites about their new life was that they could be free of sickness and disease. If you study out the Israelites journey through the wilderness, you will see that as long as they followed God's Word, no one was ever sick, weak, or diseased. They were so blessed that their clothes and shoes never even wore out! God saved them, healed them and prospered them! Don't tell me God doesn't want His people prospering. God wants His people prospering spiritually, physically, emotionally, intellectually... in every area of life.

Another redemption scripture I want you to see is found in the book of Galatians.

> *13* **Christ has redeemed us from the curse of the law, having become a curse for us (for it is written, "Cursed is everyone who hangs on a tree.")**
> **Galatians 3:13**

Christ redeemed us from the curse of the law; although, in order to understand the relevance of this scripture to God's will concerning healing, you must know the significance of the curse.

The curse that is mentioned is referring to that mentioned in Deuteronomy 28. In Deuteronomy 28, God listed the blessing and the curse. He told the Israelites that if they followed His commandments, they could walk in the blessing; if they sinned and lived in disobedience, they would walk under the curse. If you read the entire chapter, you will see the curse had to do with 3 general things: poverty, sickness, and spiritual death.

When Jesus died upon the cross, He took upon Himself the curse so we would not have to be a slave to it. Jesus became the curse for us. Jesus took poverty, sickness, and spiritual death upon Himself for the entire world.

Spiritual death could simply be defined as separation from God. It has its origin in sin; sin is what separates us from God and opens the door for death. This is what happened with Adam when he sinned against God in the Garden of Eden.

*17* For if by the one man's offense death reigned through the one, much more those who receive abundance of grace and of the gift of righteousness will reign in life through the One, Jesus Christ.

Romans 5:17

You see, because of Adam's mistake, death began to reign in this world and brought with it sickness, disease and poverty. Yet, when Jesus died, rose again and sat down at God's right hand, He broke the power of that curse over our lives. Then, when we accepted salvation, we stepped into the blessing!

*2* For the law of the Spirit of life in Christ Jesus has made me free from the law of sin and death.

Romans 8:2

We stepped out of the law of death and stepped into the law of life! We stepped into spiritual life, prosperity and HEALING! Christ redeemed us from sickness! He went through all that He did not only for your sins, but also for your sicknesses, diseases, addictions, weaknesses and malformations. Jesus wants you healed and whole, nothing missing and nothing broken.

The forgiveness of sins and healing of sicknesses is a package deal! Salvation is a wonderful package with an abundance of gifts wrapped up in it. Salvation and healing go together; you don't get one without the other!

# Chapter 13
# What Did Jesus Do?

If you want to truly see how God thinks, acts, and talks, just take a good look at Jesus. Jesus was God on the Earth; He was an exact representation of our Heavenly Father. In John 10:30, Jesus stated, "I and My Father are one." Look at something Jesus told the Jews in regards to His words and actions:

> *19* Then Jesus answered and said to them, "Most assuredly, I say to you, the Son can do nothing of Himself, but what He sees the Father do; for whatever He does, the Son also does in like manner.
> John 5:19

Do you see what He said? Jesus said that everything He said and did was because He saw God do it. So every time you see Jesus do something, you know with absolute certainty that is what God would do. Every time you see Jesus respond to a situation, you know that is how God would respond to the situation. With that truth established, let us look at the words and actions of Jesus.

## Moved With Compassion

Throughout the Gospels, we see a phrase that simply yet vividly reveals the heart of Christ and thus the heart of God: moved with compassion. There are several instances recorded for us in which we are shown Jesus love and compassion for people.

> **36 But when He saw the multitudes, He was moved with compassion for them, because they were weary and scattered, like sheep having no shepherd.**
> **Matthew 9:36**

Matthew 9:36 tells us Jesus was moved with compassion because the people truly didn't have anyone to guide them in truth. We certainly know that Jesus loves people in a general sense. We see in Matthew 9:36 that He was moved with compassion when it came to their salvation, but what about healing?

> **14 And when Jesus went out He saw a great multitude; and He was moved with compassion for them, and healed their sick.**
> **Matthew 14:14**

Jesus saw a great multitude of people and was so moved with compassion that He ministered to their sick and healed them. Remember what we just read earlier in John 5:19. Jesus only did and said what He saw God do and say. How Jesus responds to a situation is the way God would respond to a situation. Jesus knew it was God's will for these people to be healed. God's willingness combined with the people's faith brought miracles!

> **40 Now a leper came to Him, imploring Him, kneeling down to Him and saying to Him, "If You are willing, You can make me clean." 41 Then Jesus, moved with compassion, stretched out His hand and touched him, and said to him, "I**

am willing; be cleansed." 42  As soon as He had spoken, immediately the leprosy left him, and he was cleansed.

Mark 1:40-42

Again, we see Jesus moved with compassion because of someone's sickness. The result: healing power flowed. Jesus actions reflected God's heart.  God wants people healed! God wants people free of all sickness and all disease!

## Teaching, Preaching, and Healing

Once you understand that Jesus' actions and words were exactly that of God's, it makes it really easy to see God's heart, motives and responses.  If you want to get to know God, just look at Jesus!

It's interesting to me that you not only see Jesus ministering through word, but also by actions.  Not only was Jesus preaching the Good News, He was demonstrating it as well.

23  And Jesus went about all Galilee, teaching in their synagogues, preaching the gospel of the kingdom, and healing all kinds of sickness and all kinds of disease among the people.

Matthew 4:23

Jesus was teaching, preaching and healing.  He wasn't just standing behind the pulpit and delivering a message with His mouth.  He was also backing up His message with signs, wonders and miracles!

Jesus was setting people free of sickness and disease.  If this was Jesus plan, then you know it was God's plan! If this was Jesus heart, you know it was God's heart too!

> *35* Then Jesus went about all the cities and villages, teaching in their synagogues, preaching the gospel of the kingdom, and healing every sickness and every disease among the people.
>
> Matthew 9:35

Again, in Matthew 9:35 we see Jesus doing three things: teaching, preaching and healing. This was Jesus routine. Everywhere Jesus went, He was teaching, preaching and healing. He didn't do it in just some of the cities. Jesus didn't do it in God's favorite villages. It wasn't just certain cities where it was God's will for the people to be healed just like it was certain cities where it was God's will for people to be saved. Jesus went to ALL of the cities and villages, TEACHING, PREACHING AND HEALING EVERY SICKNESS AND EVER DISEASE!

## God Does The Works

> *9* Jesus said to him, "Have I been with you so long, and yet you have not known Me, Philip? He who has seen Me has seen the Father; so how can you say, 'Show us the Father'? *10* Do you not believe that I am in the Father, and the Father in Me? The words that I speak to you I do not speak on My own authority; but the Father who dwells in Me does the works. *11* Believe Me that I am in the Father and the Father in Me, or else believe Me for the sake of the works themselves.
>
> John 14:9-11

Not only was Jesus doing what He saw God do, it was God doing the works. You must understand this! Look at verse 10. Jesus said "The Father who dwells in Me does the works." In other words, every time you see Jesus heal someone, it was God healing them. Every time you see Jesus raise someone from the dead, it was God raising them from the dead. Acts 10:38 also establishes this truth.

**38 How God anointed Jesus of Nazareth with the Holy Spirit and with power, who went about doing good and healing all who were oppressed by the devil, for God was with Him.**

**Acts 10:38**

Jesus was healing people, but He wasn't doing it by Himself. Jesus was anointed by the Holy Ghost and God was with Him. In other words, you had the whole Trinity, Father, Son and Holy Spirit working together to heal people!

## Jesus Never Said No

**1 When He had come down from the mountain, great multitudes followed Him. 2 And behold, a leper came and worshiped Him, saying, "Lord, if You are willing, You can make me clean." 3 Then Jesus put out His hand and touched him, saying, "I am willing; be cleansed." Immediately his leprosy was cleansed.**

**Matthew 8:1-3**

I love this story! The leper stated, "Jesus, I know you can heal me, but I am not sure if you are willing to heal me." What was Jesus' response? I AM WILLING! And the leper was immediately healed!  Remember, if it was His will for one, it was His will for all.  God doesn't play favorites!

Although, listening to most people, they say, "You just never know what God is going to do."  That's a bunch of baloney. *I always know how God will respond to a situation.*  Some people may say that's an arrogant statement; I think it's an intelligent statement.  Why? I just look at His Word.  I look at how Jesus responded to situations and that tells me how God thinks.

In regards to healing, I always know God's heart towards people's diseases.  He wants to set them free every single time in every single situation!  In Matthew 8, Jesus established forever His willingness to heal.  If you come believing, Jesus is willing to give it to you because He has already provided it.  He can and He will!

Immediately following the healing of the leper, we again see Jesus' willingness to heal.

> **5 Now when Jesus had entered Capernaum, a centurion came to Him, pleading with Him, 6 saying, "Lord, my servant is lying at home paralyzed, dreadfully tormented." 7 And Jesus said to him, "I will come and heal him."**
>
> **Matthew 8:5-7**

Jesus was not only willing to heal the centurion's servant, He was even willing to walk to the man's house!  How many preachers do you know that would be willing to go to someone's house and pray for the sick?  I don't know of too many, but Jesus would have.  How do I know that?  Because He was willing to go to the centurion's house!  That shows you His heart for the sick. *Jesus never said no to someone who came in faith for healing.*

His ultimate desire is to see people healed of all sickness and all disease. *He was not only willing to go to someone's house to remove sickness, He was also willing to go to the cross for sickness.* Praise God He did! Hallelujah!

In the earthly ministry of Jesus, He was confronted with thousands upon thousands of people desiring healing. I would challenge you to find one instance in the Bible where Jesus turned someone down. I challenge anyone to find one instance when Jesus told someone who came for healing to go away. I challenge anyone to find an instance when Jesus told someone it was not His will to heal them.

I have never found any of these present in the Bible and I never will...because Jesus never did any of these things. Jesus always had one response: YES! All the promises of God are yes and so be it!

> *21* Now when Jesus had crossed over again by boat to the other side, a great multitude gathered to Him; and He was by the sea. *22* And behold, one of the rulers of the synagogue came, Jairus by name. And when he saw Him, he fell at His feet *23* and begged Him earnestly, saying, "My little daughter lies at the point of death. Come and lay Your hands on her, that she may be healed, and she will live." *41* Then He took the child by the hand, and said to her, "Talitha, cumi," which is translated, "Little girl, I say to you, arise." *42* Immediately the girl arose and walked, for she was twelve years of age. And they were overcome with great amazement.
> **Mark 5:21-23; 41-42**

Here is another situation in which someone came to ask Jesus for healing. The little girl wasn't even there, so Jesus went to her house. Jesus walked in, grabbed her by the hand, told her to get up and she was healed. I am telling you, Jesus wanted these people healed. If He had to walk to the other side of the city or go to another country, He would.

*If He was willing to die on the cross, I think He would be willing to walk a few miles.* Jesus wanted to reveal the nature of God to the world. He wanted people to know God loved them and cared for them. Jesus wanted people to know that God's absolute desire was to see them healed!
When people came to Jesus for healing, it didn't matter if it was one, one hundred, one thousand or a great multitude; if they wanted healing and believe they could get it, they got it!

> **23 And Jesus went about all Galilee, teaching in their synagogues, preaching the gospel of the kingdom, and healing all kinds of sickness and all kinds of disease among the people. *24* Then His fame went throughout all Syria; and they brought to Him all sick people who were afflicted with various diseases and torments, and those who were demon-possessed, epileptics, and paralytics; and He healed them.**
>
> **Matthew 4:23-24**

People came to Jesus for healing because after time, they began to see that He could and He would! You see, you can't have faith for something if you don't know you can have it. These people came expecting because they knew it was theirs for the taking.

*24* So Jesus went with him, and a great multitude followed Him and thronged Him. *25* Now a certain woman had a flow of blood for twelve years, *26* and had suffered many things from many physicians. She had spent all that she had and was no better, but rather grew worse. *27* When she heard about Jesus, she came behind Him in the crowd and touched His garment. *28* For she said, "If only I may touch His clothes, I shall be made well." *29* Immediately the fountain of her blood was dried up, and she felt in her body that she was healed of the affliction.

**Mark 5:21-29**

A woman with a blood disease came and touched Jesus. Why? Because she knew if she could just touch Him, she would be healed.  The point I want to show you is this:  Where in this situation did she ask for healing?  She didn't; she just took it!  Why?  Because she knew it was for her!  Now that is faith!

Too many people are begging, moaning, whining and praying for God to heal them, when it has already been provided. God's will is you healed!  That is why Jesus came and provided salvation...so you could be healed!  If someone living under the Old Covenant could take a healing, how much more so a child of God?

Jesus was a perfect representation of God on the Earth. When Jesus healed people, it was God healing people.  Every time Jesus said He was willing to heal - now get this - it was because He had heard God say it so many times.  Jesus said what He heard God say.  Jesus did what He saw God do. Jesus said He came to do the will of God.

**19 So Jesus explained himself at length. "I'm telling you this straight. The Son can't independently do a thing, only what he sees the Father doing. What the Father does, the Son does. The Father loves the Son and includes him in everything he is doing.**

**John 5:19 MSG**

Do you see how much weight is on this question of God's will concerning healing?  God's will is you healed.  Jesus only did the will of God.  It must be God's will for people to be healed because Jesus did a great deal of healing!  Jesus was willing because God was willing!

# Chapter 14

# Was Jesus A Confused Sinner?

This chapter title alone is enough to make you do a double take and say "What?" It almost seems blasphemous to even ask the question, but it in regards to some people's ideas regarding healing, it is a question that must be asked.

I don't know of anyone who believes that Jesus was a sinner. Even other religions outside of Christianity view Jesus a sinless person. So why in the world would I ask if Jesus was a sinner? The answer is simple.

If you believe that God's will isn't for people to be healed, then Jesus was one big sinner. Yes, you read that correctly and I will say it again. If you believe that God's will isn't for people to be healed, then Jesus was one big sinner; if that is your belief, Jesus was sinning His entire ministry on the earth!

> **9 Jesus said to him, "Have I been with you so long, and yet you have not known Me, Philip? He who has seen Me has seen the Father; so how can you say, 'Show us the Father'?**
>
> John 14:9

If God didn't want people healed, why was Jesus healing people? Everywhere Jesus went, He was teaching, preaching and healing. There are 19 individual cases of healing recorded in the Gospels. In addition to the 19 individual cases, we are told in several situations, multitudes of people were healed.

There were many places Jesus went and mass healings were taking place. If it wasn't God's will for people to be healed, then Jesus was sinning every time he ministered healing power to people because He was going against God's will.

## Was Jesus Confused?

Another thing you have to ask yourself is this: was Jesus confused? Well, if you believe God's will isn't for people to be healed, then you have to believe that Jesus was confused nutcase.

Jesus apparently thought that God's will was for people to be healed. Everywhere He went, Jesus kept healing people. Jesus stated on several occasions that He was doing God's will.

> **34  Jesus said, "The food that keeps me going is that I do the will of the One who sent me, finishing the work he started.**
>
> **John 4:34 MSG**

Jesus even believed that God was working through Him healing people!

> **9 Jesus said to him, "Have I been with you so long, and yet you have not known Me, Philip? He who**

has seen Me has seen the Father; so how can you say, 'Show us the Father'? *10* Do you not believe that I am in the Father, and the Father in Me? The words that I speak to you I do not speak on My own authority; but the Father who dwells in Me does the works. *11* Believe Me that I am in the Father and the Father in Me, or else believe Me for the sake of the works themselves.

John 14:9-11

Jesus also believed that He was doing what He saw God doing.

*19* Then Jesus answered and said to them, "Most assuredly, I say to you, the Son can do nothing of Himself, but what He sees the Father do; for whatever He does, the Son also does in like manner.

John 5:19

To make matters worse, Jesus even gave the disciples authority over sickness and disease and commanded them to heal the sick!

*1* Then He called His twelve disciples together and gave them power and authority over all demons, and to cure diseases. *2* He sent them to preach the kingdom of God and to heal the sick.

Luke 9:1-2

*1* After these things the Lord appointed seventy others also, and sent them two by two before His face into every city and place where He Himself was about to go. *8* "Whatever city you enter, and they receive you, eat such things as are set before

you. *9* And heal the sick there, and say to them,
The kingdom of God has come near to you."

Luke 10:1,8-9

*15* And He said to them, "Go into all the world and
preach the gospel to every creature... lay hands on
the sick, and they will recover."

Mark 16:15,18

So Jesus sends out the twelve disciples to heal, then sends
out seventy more disciples to heal and then sends out several
hundred to go out and heal the sick. If you believe God's will
is not for people to be healed, you are staring at a serious
dilemma here.

I mean, seriously, if you believe God's will is not for people
to be healed, you have to believe that Jesus was out of his
mind!

Jesus actually believed He saw God heal people, that God
wanted people to be healed and that God was actually
healing people through Him. If you believe God's will is not
for people to be healed, you must be way smarter than Jesus.

In my opinion, given the evidence simply revealed by the
words and actions of Jesus, it would take more faith to
believe God doesn't want people healed than to believe God
does want people healed. It's ludicrous!

I simply want you to understand that ANYONE who believes
God's will is not for people to be healed, WOULD HAVE TO
BELIEVE THAT JESUS WAS A SINNER AND JESUS WAS CONFUSED.

I on the other hand, I believe the Bible. I believe Jesus when

He said, "When you see me, you have seen the Father." When I see Jesus' heart, I see God's heart.

Jesus wasn't confused and He wasn't a sinner. Jesus was the sinless, spotless Lamb Who carried out God's will to perfection. One part of God's will was healing all those who came to Him and Jesus did just that. Look at Jesus and you see God with perfect clarity. Jesus healed people because that was, is and always will be God's will.

# Chapter 15
# The Greatest Daddy of All

How many of you want your children to be sick? No parent in their right mind would want their children to have pneumonia or allergies, much less to have cancer in their body. There is no true parent on this planet that would not want to see their sick child well. Is that not the reason for pediatricians? We have pediatricians so that loving parents can take their sick children to the doctor for treatment of illnesses.

Think of how badly it hurts you to see your children and loved ones aching, coughing, running fever, having chills, and in pain. Imagine the feeling of parents whose children are in the hospital dying of a chronic disease. Don't you think they would give anything to have their children healthy?

I know of a parent who sold their business, sold cars, took out loans, conducted fund-raisers and went into bankruptcy just trying to pay the medical bills for their sick child. They sacrificed everything so their child could be in the best cancer hospital in America enabling them to have the greatest chance of survival.

> *11* **If you then, being evil, know how to give good gifts to your children, how much more will your Father who is in heaven give good things to those who ask Him!**
>
> **Matthew 7:11**

If parents on this Earth want to give good things to their children, how much more do you think God wants to give good things to His kids? If earthly parents want their children healthy, how much more so do you think God wants His children healthy?

Think about that parent I mentioned; they sacrificed everything for their sick child to have the best of care - and they didn't even know if the results would be positive.

Think about that. How great is the love of a parent for their child! Even though these parents sacrificed a great deal, neither they nor anyone else has ever made the sacrifice that God made for us.

> **16 For God so loved the world that he gave his one and only Son, that whoever believes in him shall not perish but have eternal life.**
>
> **John 3:16**

God loved you so much that He gave. Every parent gives to their children because they love them. Love is what motivates giving. *You can give without loving, but you can't love without giving.* God gave because He loved.

Parents give to their children because of love; love is what motivates a parent to take their child to the doctor. Love is what motivates a parent to pay hundreds of dollars for prescriptions. Why? Because they don't want to see their precious children sick!

God made the greatest sacrifice anyone has ever made. God gave up His Son for the entire world, knowing that there would be some who would reject Him. He gave Jesus so we could have eternal life and become part of the family of God.

The word *life* used in John 3:16 is the Greek word *zoe*. It means "the life that belongs to God" or you could say "the God-kind of life." The very life God has is the life you receive when you accept Jesus. Is God sick? Nope. Why? Because of eternal life! That Zoe life is in you when you get into Christ! God gave you the very same life that He is so you could always be healed and whole.

> **32 He who did not spare His own Son, but delivered Him up for us all, how shall He not with Him also freely give us all things?**
>
> **Romans 8:32**

If God was willing to give us the greatest gift Heaven had to offer, don't you think He would be willing to give us anything else? Let me put it to you like this: If I gave you one thousand dollars, do you think I would have a problem giving you ten dollars? If I was willing to give a thousand, why wouldn't I be willing to give you ten dollars or even one hundred? Do you see my point? If God was willing to give us Jesus, why wouldn't He give you healing? Why wouldn't He give you finances?

God is a good God! God is a good Father! There is nothing, absolutely nothing God will withhold from you. Actually, God has it in His hand begging you to take it! He wants you to have healing! He wants you to be whole spirit, soul and body. He wants you prospering in every area of your life because He is a good Dad and He loves His children!

Every parent wants their children to have the best. I know

my parents love me very much and there is nothing they wouldn't give me if they had the opportunity or ability to do so. When we were growing up, we were not that great off financially; to be blunt, the vast majority of my childhood we were poor. All throughout my school years, we struggled financially. There were many times when we counted pennies and nickels just to go buy some milk and bread.

During those times, I know my parents went without many things just so me, my brother and sister didn't have to go without. They tried to hide it from us, but I was old enough to understand the situation we faced on a daily basis. The reason my parents sacrificed was because they loved us. The reason they tried to hide the lack of finances and the struggles was because they loved us; they didn't want us to worry.

I remember my mom working at the local mall wrapping presents during Christmas holidays. She would be up there all day, every day during the holidays after working her full-time job. Do you know why? She worked that extra job just so we could have presents under the tree. She wrapped other people's presents so we could have presents.

My mom worked that second job because she loved us. If our natural, earthly parents love us so much that they will do whatever they can to give us whatever we need, how much more so our Heavenly Father?

If our earthly parents will make sacrifices just to meet our everyday needs, how much more so will our Heavenly Father make even greater sacrifices? Matthew 6:33 states that God knows our needs. He knows our daily concerns. He watches out for us and over us because He is a good Father.

God is a great Daddy. He is the Daddy of all daddies. He isn't withholding anything from you; He has already given everything to you - He is just trying to get you to take it - all of it!

**3 Blessed be the God and Father of our Lord Jesus Christ, who has blessed us with every spiritual blessing in the heavenly places in Christ.**

**Ephesians 2:3**

God has given us everything Heaven has to offer. *If He gave you the best of Heaven, He will give you the rest of Heaven* and praise God He already has!  Healing is yours!

# Chapter 16

# Go Ye Into All The World ...And Heal?

Have you ever heard of the Great Commission? It is preached in all the churches and learned by little ones in Sunday School. It is the staple of most church's missionary programs. We have all heard it, "Go ye into all the world and preach the Gospel." The sad fact is that most people who have heard that sentence - they haven't heard the rest of the Commission.

> **15 And He said to them, "Go into all the world and preach the gospel to every creature. 16 He who believes and is baptized will be saved; but he who does not believe will be condemned. 17 And these signs will follow those who believe: In My name they will cast out demons; they will speak with new tongues; 18 they will take up serpents; and if they drink anything deadly, it will by no means hurt them; they will lay hands on the sick, and they will recover."**
>
> **Mark 16:15-18**

Did you read the last phrase? "They will lay hands on the sick and they will recover." Jesus told the disciples to go preach the Gospel. The Gospel means "good news." If someone has tumors all over their body, which is better news: "Jesus can get you to Heaven" or "Jesus can heal you?" If I am in pain and going through chemotherapy, I would smile about salvation, but I would run and dance about healing.

People need good news not only for the life to come, but also for the life they are living right now. *The great thing about salvation is that you don't have wait until your dead to start enjoying it!*

I tell you what, if you want to get someone's attention, if you want them to listen about Jesus...show them Jesus! If you want people to accept Jesus, show them how good He is and they will accept Him in a second. You see, that is what Jesus did! He went about teaching, preaching, and healing. He went about demonstrating the goodness of God. He showed people how much God loved them by healing their bodies.

When people can see Jesus will heal their body, they will accept Him as Lord and Savior! If you manifest the healing power of God, you won't have to beg people to come to Jesus...they will run you over trying to get to Him!

If it wasn't God's will for you to be healed, why would Jesus tell people to go preach the Gospel and lay hands on the sick? Again, do you see the connection between salvation and healing? They go together! Jesus wants you to tell people that He saves and He heals.

*If you believe in the Great Commission, you have to believe in healing. If you don't believe God wants people healed, then you don't believe in the Great Commission.* If a pastor doesn't believe God wants people healed, then he needs to stop preaching about the Great Commission; you can't have salvation without healing.

I want you to see something though. This was very important to Jesus and this wasn't the first time He commissioned His disciples to preach and heal.

> **1 And when he had called unto him his twelve disciples, he gave them power against unclean spirits, to cast them out, and to heal all manner of sickness and all manner of disease. 5 These twelve Jesus sent forth, and commanded them, saying, Go not into the way of the Gentiles, and into any city of the Samaritans enter ye not: 6 But go rather to the lost sheep of the house of Israel. 7 And as ye go, preach, saying, The kingdom of heaven is at hand. 8 Heal the sick, cleanse the lepers, raise the dead, cast out devils: freely ye have received, freely give.**
>
> **Matthew 10:1, 5-8**

Jesus commissioned the disciples to go preach about the Kingdom of God and heal the sick. Again, you can't have The Gospel without healing! Jesus commanded them to preach the Word, heal the sick, cast out devils and raise the dead.

Some people say, "Well, I just don't know if it is God's will to heal people;" yet, those same people will say, "Let's go on a mission trip and preach the Gospel. You know, we need to obey the Great Commission."

Would you believe that Jesus commissioned another group of people to heal the sick?

> **1 After these things the Lord appointed seventy others also, and sent them two by two before His face into every city and place where He Himself**

was about to go. *2* Then He said to them, "The harvest truly is great, but the laborers are few; therefore pray the Lord of the harvest to send out laborers into His harvest. *9* And heal the sick there, and say to them, "The kingdom of God has come near to you."

Luke 10:1-2, 9

The ministry had become so large, Jesus and the twelve disciples couldn't do it by themselves; they needed more help! So, Jesus appointed seventy others and commissioned them to preach the Gospel and heal the sick.

I know I have been repetitive with this statement, but I have to stress to you the importance of salvation and healing. They cannot be separated! Healing and the forgiveness of sins are like conjoined twins; they share the same life, the same blood, the same everything. Where one goes, the other goes.

After first commissioning the twelve disciples and then commissioning the seventy, Jesus commissioned all of His followers before He went back to Heaven.

*15* And He said to them, "Go into all the world and preach the gospel to every creature... *18* they will lay hands on the sick, and they will recover."

Mark 16:15, 18

The Great Commission is not a suggestion; it is a commandment. Jesus commanded us to go into the world and preach the Gospel to every creature - and to heal the sick.

The ministry of Jesus was too big for just Him and a few disciples.  He needed more people and that is where we come in.

> *12* "Most assuredly, I say to you, he who believes in Me, the works that I do he will do also; and greater works than these he will do, because I go to My Father.
>
> **John 14:12**

What were the works that Jesus did? Teaching, preaching and healing - and that is what He wants you to do as a Christian. If healing were not God's will, then Jesus wouldn't have given us the Great Commission.

Think about it, the very last statement Jesus made to the disciples in regards to their ministry to the world was for them to heal the sick.  People's last words are important. Jesus' last words were "Heal the sick!"

Jesus could have said all sorts of things; yet, His very last statement in Mark 16, the last phrase of the Great Commission dealt with healing.  He told them to go heal the sick.  Why? That is the heart of the Father.

God wants to see His people set free.  God wants to see His people healthy!  In essence, one of the last things Jesus said on this Earth was that God's will is you healed.

# Chapter 17

# Misconceptions About God and Healing

## 1. God teaches us through sickness.

This is a widely held belief with no Biblical backing. If you look at this statement from the standpoint of God being our Father, what Father in their right mind would discipline their child by making them sick?

If your child disobeyed you, would you ever think of exposing them to a deadly virus? No, because if you did, the government would put you in prison for a long time. If we were to do the same things we attribute to God, we would be considered child abusers!

God doesn't teach us through sickness. If He was going to put sickness on us, He would have to get it from Satan, because God doesn't have any! No, the way God teaches us is through His Word.

The vast majority of people that believe God teaches us through sickness usually base it on this scripture found in Hebrews:

> **5 And you have forgotten the exhortation which speaks to you as to sons: "My son, do not despise**

the chastening of the Lord, Nor be discouraged when you are rebuked by Him; **6** For whom the Lord loves He chastens, And scourges every son whom He receives." **7** If you endure chastening, God deals with you as with sons; for what son is there whom a father does not chasten?

**Hebrews 12:5-7**

Now, looking at Hebrews 12:6 without knowing anything else about neither God nor the Bible, I could see how people could misinterpret this scripture.    Although, did you see the phrase "the exhortation that speaks?"  It is concerning words, not destruction.  Secondly, you must understand the meaning of the word *chasten*.  If you miss this, you will miss the meaning of the whole passage.

The word *chasten* in Greek means to teach, instruct, or to train up a child.  You train a child by instructing them with words.  You teach a child their ABC's with words, not by hitting them over the head.  If you want them to know the burner on the stove is hot, you tell them; you stick their hand on it!  Just a little common sense is really all you need!  It seems to me when people get religious, they toss their brain out into the garbage.

This teaching that God teaches us with sickness is just plain old devilish.  It is a doctrine of the devil; it's as bad of a teaching as you can get!  And really, where is the common sense in this?

If someone truly believes this, I have a few questions for them.  Number one, if God is teaching people through sickness, what are they learning?  I've had people tell me

God was teaching them through their sickness. My question to them was, "What are you learning?" Their response was usually, "I don't know." Some will say they are learning patience. Yeah, that makes a lot of sense too. I don't have to hold my hand on a hot stove for five minutes enduring excruciating pain to learn patience. I can learn patience and obedience and anything else without pain and suffering.

My second question is this: what is a sick child learning? I mean, if God teaches us through sickness, what in the world is a two year old with leukemia learning? Seriously, it's ridiculous theological thinking and an outright horrible accusation against God.

My third question is regarding those who have had accidents and as a result had a life altering injury such as losing a limb or becoming paralyzed. I know of someone who broke their neck diving into shallow water and as a result became a paraplegic. Did God push them into the shallow water or because of carelessness, were they the fault of the accident? Is someone injuring themselves part of God's plan? No. Is it His will? No. Is God teaching them something through it? No!

Actually, the Bible says that the Holy Spirit is our Guide and Revealer; He isn't guiding us into tragedy; instead, He is warning us and trying to guide us away from tragedy. He leads us into the blessing, not the curse.

If God allows us or causes us to go through accidental injuries so we can learn, why don't we all dive into a shallow pond? Why don't we all slam our car into a tree hoping to get injured so we can learn more about God. Again, the more you talk about it, the more absurd it becomes.

Finally, if God teaches through sickness, shouldn't we all be begging God to make us sick so we can get smart?  Yet, looking at that question, doesn't that sound stupid?  Uh, yeah.  But seriously, all those people in the hospital trying to get well and all the people taking medications to deal with varying sickness and disease - shouldn't they stop trying to get better so they can learn more?  Shouldn't the sickest people on the planet be the smartest people on the planet?  I don't think so.  It's simply foolish.

Remember, God good; devil bad.  That simple statement will keep you from foolish teachings!

> **4 And you, fathers, do not provoke your children to wrath, but bring them up in the training and admonition of the Lord.**
>
> **Ephesians 6:4**

The word *training* is the same Greek word translated *chasten* used in Hebrews 12.  Obviously, this is quite a bit different from our ideas of chastening.  We are not talking about sending calamity and destruction.  You don't put sickness on a child to teach them; that's child abuse!

Let's look at another scripture that will shed more light on this topic.

> **16 All Scripture is given by inspiration of God, and is profitable for doctrine, for reproof, for correction, for instruction in righteousness.**
>
> **2 Timothy 3:16**

The same Greek word translated *chasten* is the same word translated *instruction* in this verse.  So, if you go back and read Hebrews 12:5 with this understanding, it is easy to see exactly what He is talking about.

> **5 And you have forgotten the exhortation which speaks to you as to sons: "My son, do not despise the chastening (instruction) of the Lord, Nor be discouraged when you are rebuked by Him.**
>
> **Hebrews 12:5**

I want to point out something quite interesting to you. Notice that this scripture is referring to God dealing with His children. *If you interpret this scripture that God chastens His children with sickness, then it would mean that no sinner would ever be sick.* No sinners would ever have any problems, they would never face destruction in their lives, and they would never be sick. We know this is not true, but this is the absurdity that must be true if you believe God teaches His children with sickness.

Another reason we misunderstand Hebrews 12:5 is because we are looking at it from a physical, natural standpoint. Our earthly Father is a man, so he teaches and instructs us through natural means. Our Heavenly Father is a spirit and He teaches and instructs us through spiritual means.

You must understand that we are a spirit, we have a soul (our mind, will, and emotions) and we live in a body. (I would highly suggest reading Kenneth E. Hagin's book on this subject *The Three Dimensions of Man*.) God deals with our spirits. He talks to us by our spirit.

The way God instructs us is through His Word. Remember 2 Timothy 3:16? It is His Word that is profitable for instruction. It is His Word that chastens us. Did you ever see in the Bible where it said that sickness was profitable for correction and instruction? No! What we do see used for correction and instruction is the Word of God. God teaches, chastens, corrects and reproves us through His Word.

## 2. God gets glory by our being sick.

This is a classic belief inspired by Satan himself and it is widespread all over the world. Because of the misinterpretation of two passages of scripture, this belief has held people in bondage in believing that God wants them sick.

> *1* Now as Jesus passed by, He saw a man who was blind from birth. *2* And His disciples asked Him, saying, "Rabbi, who sinned, this man or his parents, that he was born blind?" *3* Jesus answered, "Neither this man nor his parents sinned, but that the works of God should be revealed in him. *4* I must work the works of Him who sent Me while it is day; the night is coming when no one can work.
>
> John 9:1-4

During Jesus' time on the earth, it was believed that if someone was sick, diseased, malformed, etc, it was due to sin in their life or sin in their parent's life. This is why the disciples asked Jesus, "Who sinned, this man or his parents?" Of course, verse three is where most people have screwed this all up, although the translators didn't help much either. John 9:3 says, **"Neither this man nor his parents sinned, but that the works of God should be revealed in him."**

Now, if I am looking at this verse and only this verse, it would be very easy to understand why many people believe God wanted this man sick so He could get glory out of healing him. Yet, common sense tells me that is stupid! Why would God make someone sick so He could heal them? That is one of the dumbest things I have ever heard and yet it is an accepted teaching in churches all over the planet.

Let me give you an illustration. What if you went to a magic show and the magician was doing the classic "rabbit in the hat" trick. Now, normally, they show you an empty hat, wave their wand and pull the rabbit out of the hat. Well, that will get some applause. But what if the magician initially showed you the rabbit, then put the rabbit in the hat, waved their wand and then pulled the rabbit back out of the hat? The entire audience would let out a big "BOOOOOO!!!" Why?

How can you get glory and praise for taking something out of a hat that you just put in? Anyone can do that; it would be absolutely ludicrous for a magician to do that - yet, this is what we attribute to God.

People believe based off of this scripture that God makes people sick so He can take it off and then receive praise from humanity. That is just plain stupid! God gets praise for healing someone on whom Satan has placed sickness. Let's take a look at John 9:3-4 again.

> **3 Jesus answered, "Neither this man nor his parents sinned, but that the works of God should be revealed in him. 4 I must work the works of Him who sent Me while it is day; the night is coming when no one can work.**
>
> **John 9:3-4**

You must understand that in the Greek, there is no punctuation. When the translators of the Bible translated the New Testament from Greek to English, they were the ones who put the periods, colons, semicolons, question marks, etc, in the text. So based on their understanding of what was being said, they chose where the punctuation marks were to be placed.

With that being said, I want to point out something to you. Look at Jesus statement in verse three. If you take out the comma after the phrase "parents sinned" and replace it with a period, and replace the period after "should be revealed in him" with a comma, then those two verses take on a completely new meaning.

If you paid attention in English class, you know that a simple punctuation mark can change the meaning of a sentence. Look at verses 3 and 4 with the proposed change in punctuation and the new meaning that follows.

> *3* Jesus answered, "Neither this man nor his parents sinned." *4* "But that the works of God should be revealed in Him, *I* must work the works of Him who sent Me while it is day..."
>
> John 9:3-4

Do you see it? In order for God to get glory out of this situation, Jesus had to work the works of God in the blind man. Another words, Jesus had to heal the man for God to get glory. God didn't make the man blind, but He did make the man to see because in John 9:7, the blind man was healed! Glory to God!

There is one more scripture that people use to show that

God uses sickness for His glory and I want to make sure we address this one as well. It is found in the story of Lazarus.

> *1* Now a certain man was sick, Lazarus of Bethany, the town of Mary and her sister Martha. *2* It was that Mary who anointed the Lord with fragrant oil and wiped His feet with her hair, whose brother Lazarus was sick. *3* Therefore the sisters sent to Him, saying, "Lord, behold, he whom You love is sick." *4* When Jesus heard that, He said, "This sickness is not unto death, but for the glory of God, that the Son of God may be glorified through it."
>
> John 11:1-4

Notice verse four. People have taken this statement along with John 9:3 about the blind man and have made a doctrine that God uses sickness of His glory. This is simply not true.

Look carefully at the context of what Jesus was saying. He wasn't saying that God put sickness on Lazarus so God could take it off and get praise. Jesus said He was going to get glory through it.

Take a look at the Message Translation which did a far better job of conveying the truth in this passage of scripture.

> *1* A man was sick, Lazarus of Bethany, the town of Mary and her sister Martha. *2* This was the same Mary who massaged the Lord's feet with aromatic oils and then wiped them with her hair. It was her brother Lazarus who was sick. *3* So the sisters sent word to Jesus, "Master, the one you love so very much is sick." *4* When Jesus got the message, he said, "This sickness is not fatal. It will become an

**occasion to show God's glory by glorifying God's Son."**

**John 11:1-4 MSG**

This was just another opportunity to reveal the power of God! This was just another opportunity to reveal the love of God! This was another opportunity for Jesus to establish that He was indeed the Son of God. Anytime something bad has happened, it is always an opportunity for someone who knows God's power to intervene in the situation.

I've never seen anyone give God glory for someone becoming sick or dying; although, there are numerous passages of scripture in the Bible where people are healed, delivered and set free and the people give God glory and praise!

Remember, in situations like these where the understanding of the scripture may seem a little fuzzy - always go back to John 10:10 and Acts 10:38. Do you remember these two scriptures by now?

> **10 The thief does not come except to steal, and to kill, and to destroy. I have come that they may have life, and that they may have it more abundantly.**
>
> 
>
> **John 10:10**
>
> 

Think about it. In John 9, the blind man was healed. In John 10, Jesus explained where sickness comes from. In John 11 is the story of Lazarus being raised from the dead. Keep things in context!

I have another question for you? If God gets glory out of making His people sick, what does that say about Him? If you put Hepatitis C on your kids, how many people do you think would give you a standing ovation? None, but there would be a lot of people wanting to kill you! Let's use some common sense. Use the brain that God gave you!

So who kills, who brings sickness, who brings disease? Satan. Who brings life, raises people from the dead and heals people of all sickness and disease? Jesus. Remember: God good. Devil bad.

> **38 How God anointed Jesus of Nazareth with the Holy Spirit and with power, who went about doing good and healing all who were oppressed by the devil, for God was with Him.**
>
> **Acts 10:38**

Again, who was doing the healing? Jesus! Who was making people sick? The devil. Keep those two verses always in the forefront and you will never have any problems with understanding the Bible. God good; devil bad. God's will is you healed. He isn't making you sick, He isn't getting glory out of you being sick, He doesn't enjoy seeing you suffer. If it was His will for people to be sick, then people need to stop going to the hospital trying to get well.

## 3.  I'm suffering for Jesus with my sickness

All these people who sit there and say God wants them to suffer with sickness - if they can afford it, they are taking prescriptions trying to get well. Does that even make sense?

If this is the case, all hospitals need to close their doors and all medical professionals need to find another profession.

Why? *If it is God's will for people to be sick and share in Christ's sufferings, then all medical professional are working against God.* If you believe God made you sick so you can suffer, then why are you going to the doctor and trying to hinder God's plan? If you believe this, you are sinning against God because He's trying to keep you sick and you are trying to get better!

Now, there is a legitimacy to suffering for Christ. There are actually many scriptures in the Bible that talk explicitly about this subject. Yet, again as with all things, you have to keep scripture in context. Don't go off of what someone said about suffering for Jesus; look at what the Bible has to say on the subject.

> **19 For this is commendable, if because of conscience toward God one endures grief, suffering wrongfully.**
> **1 Peter 2:19**

> **12 As many as desire to make a good showing in the flesh, these would compel you to be circumcised, only that they may not suffer persecution for the cross of Christ.**
> **Galatians 6:12**

You will find that the references to suffering refer to persecution from people. Jesus' sacrifice redeemed us from a lot of things - but He didn't deliver us from people. Whether it is in regard to verbal persecution or physical, the scripture references you will find always deal with people.

> **16 For his Holy Spirit speaks to us deep in our hearts and tells us that we are God's children. 17 And since we are his children, we will share his treasures --**

for everything God gives to his Son, Christ, is ours, too. But if we are to share his glory, we must also share his suffering. *18* Yet what we suffer now is nothing compared to the glory he will give us later.

**Romans 8:16-18  NLT**

You will find the apostle Paul talked a great deal about suffering and persecution. In Romans 8:16-18, Paul explicitly says that we are to share in Christ's suffering. Now let me ask you a question. Did you ever read where Jesus was sick? Did you ever see where Jesus suffered any type of sickness or disease? No; although, we do see where Jesus suffered an abundance of persecution from people because of His faith.

So we know Jesus never suffered any type of sickness or disease, yet Paul tells us that we are to share in Christ's sufferings. In 2 Corinthians, Paul gives us a list of all the things he has suffered for the sake of the Gospel.

*23* **Are they servants of Christ? I can go them one better. (I can't believe I'm saying these things. It's crazy to talk this way! But I started, and I'm going to finish.)** *24* **I've been flogged five times with the Jews' thirty-nine lashes,** *25* **beaten by Roman rods three times, pummeled with rocks once. I've been shipwrecked three times, and immersed in the open sea for a night and a day.** *26* **In hard traveling year in and year out, I've had to ford rivers, fend off robbers, struggle with friends, struggle with foes. I've been at risk in the city, at risk in the country, endangered by desert sun and sea storm, and betrayed by those I thought were my brothers.** *27* **I've known drudgery and hard labor, many a long and lonely night without sleep, many a missed**

> meal, blasted by the cold, naked to the weather. *28*
> **And that's not the half of it, when you throw in the
> daily pressures and anxieties of all the churches.
> *29* When someone gets to the end of his rope, I
> feel the desperation in my bones. When someone
> is duped into sin, an angry fire burns in my gut. *30*
> If I have to "brag" about myself, I'll brag about the
> humiliations that make me like Jesus.**
> 2 Corinthians 11:20-30  MSG

Did you notice in everything Paul listed, sickness was not one of them?  Although you may see a mention of someone being sick, you will never find Paul nor any other writer refer to sickness or disease as one of their "sufferings."

God doesn't want you to suffer with sickness; He wants you to prosper!  His will is you healed.  His will is you whole.  God gave us doctors!  God gave us wisdom regarding our bodies!  God gave us knowledge about medications.  He is a good God, and a good Father.  His ultimate desire is to see you well in your body!  He has sacrificed everything in order for you to have healing.  God's will is you healed...case closed!

## 4.  Paul's Thorn

The subject of Paul's thorn in the flesh has been misused and abused by so many Christians.  Satan has twisted this scripture and used it to deceive multitudes into thinking God wanted them to have some type of sickness or disease.

> **7 And lest I should be exalted above measure by the
> abundance of the revelations, a thorn in the flesh
> was given to me, a messenger of Satan to buffet**

me, lest I be exalted above measure. *8 Concerning this thing I pleaded with the Lord three times that it might depart from me. 9 And He said to me, "My grace is sufficient for you, for My strength is made perfect in weakness."* Therefore most gladly I will rather boast in my infirmities, that the power of Christ may rest upon me.

**2 Corinthians 12:7-9**

This thorn came because of the abundance of revelations Paul had received.  In the beginning of 2 Corinthians 12, Paul tells us that God even took him to Heaven and revealed some wonderful things to him.  Until you have an abundance of revelations, you are not going to have a thorn - this would disqualify the vast majority of Christians claiming to have a "thorn."

Secondly, we must first understand that God has no problem with us being exalted.  God wants us to be exalted and promoted in the eyes of other people for His glory, but there is a right way and a wrong way.  Many people have said God was trying to keep Paul from being prideful so God made Him sick.  In 1 Peter, 5:6 we are told "God exalts the humble."

Satan does not want us exalted before people.  Paul was not speaking of himself being exalted above measure because of pride, but rather the thorn came from Satan trying to keep God from exalting his influence and ministry.  When we grow in the things of God, God promotes us and our influence increases, that creates more havoc for Satan.

We also need to understand that this "thorn" was not any type of sickness.  People have tried to argue that Paul's thorn was a eye disease by taking statements Paul made and taking them out of context. Let's look at the scriptures that have been used to try and justify this belief.

> 13 You know that because of physical infirmity I preached the gospel to you at the first. 14 And my trial which was in my flesh you did not despise or reject, but you received me as an angel of God, even as Christ Jesus. 15 What then was the blessing you enjoyed? For I bear you witness that, if possible, you would have plucked out your own eyes and given them to me.
>
> Galatians 4:13-15

In reading this passage of scripture and putting it together with 2 Corinthians 12, I can see how some people have supposed Paul was made sick with an eye disease. The problem is you need to look at who Paul was speaking to when he wrote this. Paul was speaking to the church at Galatia. In Acts 14, Paul was stoned and left for dead in the Lystra, which was a city of Galatia. The next day Paul walked to Derbe, which was another city of Galatia. I am sure Paul had lots of cuts, bumps and bruises; maybe his eyes were swollen from getting hit with rocks!

Another verse that is used to justify the belief that Paul's thorn was a sickness, and more specifically an eye disease, is found in Galatians 6.

> 11 See with what large letters I have written to you with my own hand! 12 As many as desire to make a good showing in the flesh, these would compel you to be circumcised, only that they may not suffer persecution for the cross of Christ.
>
> Galatians 6:11-12

People have tried to say Paul wrote with large writing because he couldn't see well due to the eye disease.  That's a pretty big stretch!  It is a lot easier and more credible to believe Paul was referring to the long letter(s) he had written to the Galatian church.

The third scripture used to justify that Paul's thorn was a sickness or disease is found at the end of our original passage of study.

> **7 And lest I should be exalted above measure by the abundance of the revelations, a thorn in the flesh was given to me, a messenger of Satan to buffet me, lest I be exalted above measure. 8 Concerning this thing I pleaded with the Lord three times that it might depart from me. 9 And He said to me, "My grace is sufficient for you, for My strength is made perfect in weakness." Therefore most gladly I will rather boast in my infirmities, that the power of Christ may rest upon me.**
>
> **2 Corinthians 12:7-9**

At the end of verse 9, Paul states that, "I will rather boast in my infirmities..."  The word *infirmities* can mean sickness, but it also means lack or inadequacy.  For example, Romans 8:26 tell us "the Spirit also helpeth our infirmities."  It context, it is not telling us the Holy Spirit helps us with sicknesses, but that many times we don't know how to pray for certain things.

What really clears this up for us is that just a few verses before in 2 Corinthians 11, Paul uses the phrase "boast in my infirmities" and is referring to all of the persecutions he endured.

**23 Are they ministers of Christ?—I speak as a fool—I am more: in labors more abundant, in stripes above measure, in prisons more frequently, in deaths often. 24 From the Jews five times I received forty stripes minus one. 25 Three times I was beaten with rods; once I was stoned; three times I was shipwrecked; a night and a day I have been in the deep; 26 in journeys often, in perils of waters, in perils of robbers, in perils of my own countrymen, in perils of the Gentiles, in perils in the city, in perils in the wilderness, in perils in the sea, in perils among false brethren; 27 in weariness and toil, in sleeplessness often, in hunger and thirst, in fastings often, in cold and nakedness— 28 besides the other things, what comes upon me daily: my deep concern for all the churches. 29 Who is weak, and I am not weak? Who is made to stumble, and I do not burn with indignation? 30 If I must boast, I will boast in the things which concern my infirmity.**

**2 Corinthians 11:23-30**

Again, Paul wasn't talking about sickness or disease. He was referring to the persecutions he endured; he never mentioned any type of sickness or disease, including the popularly preached "eye disease."

So what was the thorn in the flesh? If you read all of verse 2 Corinthians 12:7, we find out the thorn in the flesh was "a messenger of Satan to buffet me." The messenger of Satan was not a disease, but literally a demon sent to buffet Paul.

Again, you must interpret scripture with scripture. There are three other instances in the Bible where phrases such as "thorns in your side" and "thorns in your eyes" are used and they verify the meaning of Paul's thorn in the flesh.

**35 But if you do not drive out the inhabitants of the land from before you, then it shall be that those whom you let remain shall be irritants in your eyes and thorns in your sides, and they shall harass you in the land where you dwell.**

**Numbers 33:35**

**13 know for certain that the LORD your God will no longer drive out these nations from before you. But they shall be snares and traps to you, and scourges on your sides and thorns in your eyes, until you perish from this good land which the LORD your God has given you.**

**Joshua 23:13**

**3 Therefore I also said, 'I will not drive them out before you; but they shall be thorns in your side, and their gods shall be a snare to you.'**

**Judges 2:3**

In all three instances, these "thorns" were never sickness and disease; instead, the "thorns" were descriptive of persecution the people would endure.

So quite simply, Paul's thorn was not a sickness; the thorn was dealing with persecution by people being influenced by a demon, a messenger of Satan. Satan was causing the persecution (thorn), not God. Satan was simply trying to hinder Paul's influence and ministry from increasing.

# Study Guide

## CHAPTER ONE - Where Did You Get Those Beliefs
1. Our beliefs are to be based and founded upon _____?
2. What does John 6:63 say?
3. Are there any areas of your life where you think your beliefs may be influenced more by opinion than the Word of God?
4. What are your current beliefs regarding healing?

## CHAPTER TWO - I Know You Can But Will You
1. What passage of scripture in Matthew did Jesus state He was willing to heal?
2. Most people believe God can heal, but wonder if He ___?
3. What did Jesus do that showed His unwavering willingness to heal and His compassion for the sick?
4. It is not enough to know God's _____; you must also know His _____.
5. Is there an area of your life where you have wondered if God would provide for you?

## CHAPTER THREE - God Good. Devil Bad
1. What is an easy way to remember where good and evil comes from?
2. What two scriptures plainly show God's actions and Satan's actions?
3. Who is the author of sickness, disease, death and destruction?

4. What does James 1:17 say?

5. Can you remember a situation in which you wondered if the negative circumstances you were experiencing were from God? Why did you feel/think that way?

## CHAPTER FOUR - In The Beginning

1. Everything God made in creation was _____?

2. Where in the creation account did God create sickness and disease?

3. Man was made in the image of _____ and was made to be _____?

4. Reflect on how God made the earth and made man. Think about what God placed in man and how He made man to be just like Him.

## CHAPTER FIVE - God's Will In Heaven

1. Where in the Bible did Jesus pray, "Your will be done on earth as it is in Heaven?"

2. Is there any sickness or disease in Heaven?

3. From what you see in the Bible, what is God's will on the earth?

4. Reflect on what Heaven is like and how your life would be without sickness. Now imagine yourself living like that on the earth.

## CHAPTER SIX - The Origin of Sickness

1. How did sickness get into the earth?

2. What was the result of Adam's sin?

3. How do you get darkness?

4. Think about the information you've learned in this chapter and how it relates to what you have been taught in the past about where sickness comes from. Does it contradict what you learned in the past? How so?

## CHAPTER SEVEN - Old Testament Symbols
1.  What is a type/shadow refer to in the Bible?
2.  What are two symbols in the Old Testament that show God's will concerning healing?  Where are these symbols referenced in the Bible?
3.  With what situation did Jesus compare Himself to in John 3:14?
4.  Think about how the story of the Passover Lamb relates to communion.  Talk about the correlation between the two and how communion symbolizes God's will concerning the forgiveness of sin and the healing of our bodies.

## CHAPTER EIGHT - God's First A.K.A.
1.  What was the first name God used to reveal Himself to the Israelites after they were delivered from Egypt?
2.  Explain why people have used Exodus 15:26 as evidence that God puts sickness on people.
3.  What are some of the other names God used to reveal Himself throughout the Old Testament?
4.  Meditate on God's redemptive name Jehovah Rophe, The Lord Who Heals.  In light of what your current beliefs are regarding healing, how does this name affect your beliefs?

## CHAPTER NINE - Rich, Healthy Job
1.  What two reasons are why most people misunderstand the story of Job?
2.  What was Job doing that opened the door for Job's suffering?
3.  Who brought the destruction in Job's life? What scripture reference in Job proves this?
4.  Do you see how the story of Job has been misinterpreted and misconstrued?  How would you explain Job's story to someone who is using Job's suffering as an excuse for their situation?

## CHAPTER TEN - Is Healing For All Or Just For Some

1. Name two scriptures that prove God does not show favoritism.
2. True or false: all of the people healed in the Old Testament and in Jesus earthly ministry were sinners.
3. Name three passages of scripture in which "Jesus healed them all."
4. Reread all of the passages of scripture that refer to Jesus healing all sickness and all disease for all of the people. If you are facing a health issue right now, begin to meditate on the truth that you are included in "all people" and the sickness you are dealing with is included in "all sickness and all disease."

## CHAPTER ELEVEN - If It Isn't God's Will To Heal All

1. If people believe it isn't God's will for them to be healed, explain why they would be in sin for taking medication in order to get better.
2. Which one of the questions/statements listed in this chapter stands out to you the most? Why?
3. If Jesus was going against God's will in that Jesus was healing people, what would be the result?
4. Think of another question along these lines that you could ask someone that believes God's will is for people to be sick.

## CHAPTER TWELVE - The Salvation Package

1. The Greek and Hebrew word for salvation implies what five meanings; what are they?
2. What Old Testament passage of scripture is quoted by Matthew and Peter in reference to what Jesus did for us on the cross?
3. Name two scriptures that show the relationship of the forgiveness of sin and healing of disease.
4. By gaining a better and fuller understanding of salvation,

how does it now affect your view of healing?

## CHAPTER THIRTEEN- What Did Jesus Do
1. If you want to see what God would do, look at _____?
2. How did Jesus words and actions reflect God's will for humanity?
3. Name two passages of scripture in which Jesus healed an individual.
4. Think about Jesus words and actions regarding healing. How does that affect your view of God?

## CHAPTER FOURTEEN - Was Jesus A Confused Sinner
1. Jesus stated He represented who?
2. Jesus said His food was to _____?
3. What would be the result of Jesus actually sinning against God?
4. Think about how many people believe God wants people sick and then relate that to what Jesus was doing on the earth. How would you explain the statements in this chapter to someone who believes God's will is not healing?

## CHAPTER FIFTEEN - The Greatest Daddy Of All
1. Where in the Bible is the following scripture found: "If you then being evil know how to give good gifts to your children, how much more will your Father who is in heaven give good things to those who ask Him."
2. You can give without loving, but you can't love_____?
3. What is the meaning of the Greek word *zoe*?
4. In Ephesians 2:3 we are told that our Heavenly Father blessed us with all spiritual blessings in Christ. Spend a few minutes meditating on that truth. How does it help you in your view of God's desire for you to be healthy?

## CHAPTER SIXTEEN - Go Ye Into All The World...And Heal

1. What are the four signs Jesus said would follow those who believe?

2. If you believe in the Great Commission, you must believe _____.

3. What are the three scripture references where Jesus commissioned people to heal the sick?

4. Think about John 14:12. What does this statement mean to you? How does it affect your view of the Great Commission?

## CHAPTER SEVENTEEN - Misconceptions About God and Healing

1. What New Testament scripture do many people use to prove that God teaches us with sickness?

2. What does the word *chasten* mean? What two other words in the English language are the same Greek word for *chasten*?

3. According to Hebrews 12:5, if God chastens His children with sickness, then it would mean that no _____ would ever be sick.

4. According to the Bible, what does God use to teach us?

5. Discuss what Paul's thorn was and why it was in Paul's life.

# Prayer for Salvation and Baptism of the Holy Spirit

It is the desire of God that everyone accept His free gift of salvation. God sent the greatest gift Heaven had so the world could be set free; that precious gift was Jesus! Despite knowing the mistakes you would make, He still climbed up on the cross. Why? His love was greater than your sin.

Romans 10:9, 10 says if you will confess Jesus as your Lord and Savior and believe that He arose from the dead, you will saved. You see, salvation has nothing to do with works. It doesn't matter what church you belong to, how many little old ladies you help across the street or how much you give the church. You can not earn salvation, you can not buy salvation; you must simply accept salvation.

Another free gift God has provided is the Baptism of the Holy Spirit. In Acts 2, we find this second gift being given to the Church. God desires that you be filled with His Spirit with the evidence of speaking in tongues.

God said in Acts 2:38 that this life changing gift was for everyone, not just a select few. It was not set aside for just the 12 disciples nor the early Church; it was given for all who would accept His precious Son Jesus! The infilling of the Holy Spirit will allow you to operate in the fullness of God's power and be a blessing to the entire world.

If you have never accepted Jesus as your Lord and Savior or accepted God's gift of being filled with the Holy Spirit, I invite you to pray the following prayer:

*Father, I believe that you sent Jesus to the earth just for me. I believe that He died on the cross and arose from the dead. I confess Him as my Savior and accept Him as Lord over my life. I thank you that by His sacrifice, my sins have been forgiven and I am a new creature in Christ Jesus! I am now your child!*

*I now ask you for the infilling of the Holy Spirit with the evidence of speaking in tongues. You said in Your Word it was a gift, so I ask You for it and receive it right now. I thank you for my heavenly language.*

*Thank you for your mercy! Thank you for being in love with me! Thank you for being my Father! Thank you for being so good to me!*

We encourage you to become involved in a solid, Bible-based church. Begin praying in the Spirit daily and spend time reading your Bible. Now it is time to start growing in the Lord - and don't forget to tell someone about what Jesus did for you! Remember, God is good and He has good things in store for you!

If you prayed this prayer or this book has impacted your life in any way, we would like to hear from you!

Please visit us on the web at: www.ChadGonzales.com

## Other books by Chad Gonzales

Aliens
Fearless: Living life the way God intended
Making Right Decisions
The Freedom of Forgiveness
Walking In The Miraculous - A 30 Day Devotional
What's Next?